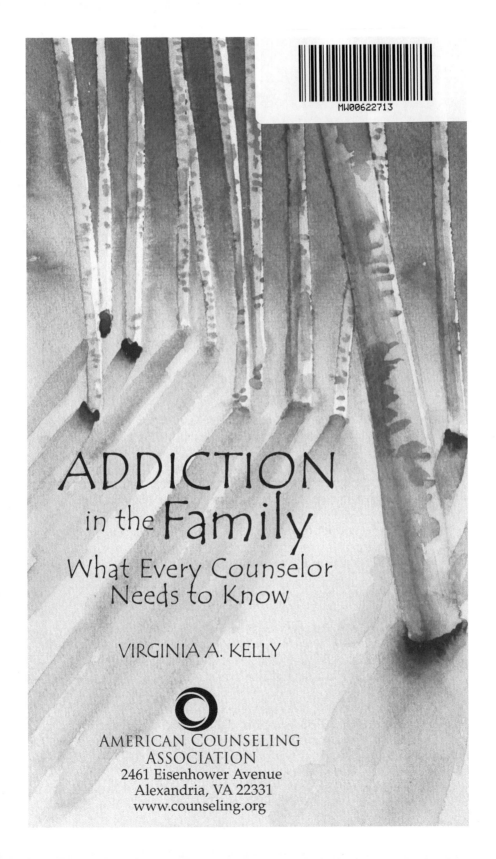

ADDICTION
in the Family
What Every Counselor Needs to Know

VIRGINIA A. KELLY

AMERICAN COUNSELING
ASSOCIATION
2461 Eisenhower Avenue
Alexandria, VA 22331
www.counseling.org

MW00622713

ADDICTION
in the Family
What Every Counselor
Needs to Know

American Counseling Association
2461 Eisenhower Avenue • Alexandria, VA 22331

Associate Publisher • Carolyn C. Baker

Digital and Print Development Editor • Nancy Driver

Production Manager • Bonny E. Gaston

Copy Editor • Kimberly W. Kinne

Cover and text design by Bonny E. Gaston

Library of Congress Cataloging-in-Publication Data
Kelly, Virginia A.
   Addiction in the family: what every counselor needs to know/ Virginia A. Kelly, Fairfield University.
      pages cm
   Includes bibliographical references and index.
   ISBN 978-1-55620-334-3 (pbk. : alk. paper)   1. Drug abuse counseling.   2. Alcoholism counseling.   3. Substance abuse—Treatment.   I. Title.
   RC564.K464 2015
   362.29'186—dc23   2015023236

This book is dedicated to the memory of
Marilyn Teresa Murphy Ruocco,
my first and best teacher!

CONTENTS

Contents

PREFACE

This book is written for counselors and counselors-in-training. The issues of substance use and abuse are inescapable and extend to clients in every setting. Although there are textbooks that target working with individuals who have a substance use disorder (SUD), there is no such resource for understanding how this issue affects those closest to the person with the disorder. This book has been written to fill that gap.

The book covers some pertinent basics, including definitions, history, etiological models, and commonly abused substances. After going over the basics, I discuss the theoretical frameworks from which the counselor can conceptualize the issue of living in a family with someone who has an SUD. Specifically, family theory and developmental theory are covered and applied to this population of clients. Codependency is then described as a single construct that has been used to characterize the population of clients who have lived with family members struggling with an SUD. The emotional, relational, and behavioral consequences of familial SUD are explored as well as the multicultural implications of working with this group of clients. Finally, I describe and apply a number of treatment modalities.

ABOUT THE AUTHOR

Virginia A. Kelly, PhD, LPC, is an associate professor in the Department of Counselor Education at Fairfield University in Fairfield, Connecticut. She teaches a variety of courses, including Substance Abuse in the Family. Ginny also maintains a private practice, where she works with adolescents, adults, and couples.

Ginny received her doctorate in counselor education from the University of North Carolina at Greensboro, her master's degree in counselor education from The Pennsylvania State University, and her bachelor of arts degree from the State University of New York at Geneseo. Ginny has published articles in the areas of substance abuse, spirituality, psychological abuse, and program-level assessment. She has also coedited a book, *Critical Incidents in Addictions Counseling,* and most recently coedited *Critical Incidents in Integrating Spirituality Into Counseling.*

ACKNOWLEDGMENTS

I want to thank Carolyn Baker and Nancy Driver for their dedication to this project. Your editorial support was invaluable. In addition, I would like to thank Ellie Hawthorne, daughter of Earl and Hilagund Brinkman, who awarded me funds to begin this project from the Brinkman Private Charitable Foundation. To the students who so willingly assisted me in creating case examples and served as my test case as I tried out parts of this manuscript—Alexis, Kara, Melissa, Mindy, Marian, Brittanni, Frank, Jessica, Giovanna, Erin, and Marlena—thank you. And to Marian Boyns, who worked with me for countless hours, conducting research, editing, and even providing food when necessary, I want to express my heartfelt thanks. To my colleagues at Fairfield University, Drs. Diana Hulse, Tracey Robert, and Bogusia Skudzryk, thank you for your support and encouragement.

Most important, I need to thank my family. My amazing parents, Joe and Marilyn, who taught us all about family and love. To my siblings, Joey (especially Joey!), Robert, Mary, Chris, Peter, and Timmy, for keeping me grounded and for choosing such wonderful partners who have enriched all of our lives (Lisa, Craig, Melissa, and Tara). To my amazing nieces and nephews, who remain solidly connected, maintaining the bond. And to my wonderful daughter-in-law, Kathy, and my perfect granddaughter, Maia—I am so grateful to have both of you in my life. To my children, Drew and Charlie, who taught me everything about love and family and life: I am so proud to be your mother! And finally, thank you to Mike Wallace for your endless support, encouragement, and belief in me. I cannot imagine life without you in my corner.

To all of the countless colleagues and students I have had along the way: Each one of you has touched my life. And to my clients: I am humbled and honored to have shared in your journeys of healing, and I am forever grateful for all that you have taught me. This book is a tribute to you!

INTRODUCTION

Every counselor in every setting will encounter the issues of substance use and abuse. The universality of these issues is well established (National Council on Alcoholism and Drug Dependence, Inc. [NCADD], n.d.-a), and addiction and substance use disorder (SUD) cross all known boundaries. In addition, the scope and impact of this issue is extensive. It is estimated that one in every 12 adults struggles with alcohol abuse or dependence, and an estimated 20 million Americans (approximately 8% of the population) used an illegal drug within the past 30 days (NCADD, n.d.-c). These represent the data pertaining specifically to those who have an SUD themselves. These numbers in no way capture the true impact of this issue, as it extends well beyond the individual who has the disorder.

It is estimated that more than half of all adults have a family history of alcoholism, and more than 7 million children live with a parent who abuses alcohol (Dunn et al., 2002; NCADD, n.d.-b.). The counseling profession has its roots in an understanding that environments affect clients. In particular, it is well established that the perceived quality of people's closest relationships has tremendous influence on their sense of overall well-being (American Counseling Association [ACA], 2009). It is therefore important that counselors in all settings develop an understanding of how SUD affects those individuals who are closest to the person with the disorder. There is a body of knowledge pertaining to this phenomenon, and this book was written to synthesize that knowledge in a manner that will enable professional counselors to apply what is known to their work with clients who have been affected by close relationships with substance-abusing individuals.

About This Book

My purpose with this book is to address the specific issues that seem to surface for individuals who live with a family member who has an SUD. As with any issue, the individual client profiles differ. This book uses case examples as a means of illustrating the manifestation of the issues covered throughout the literature. The clients in these case studies are primarily fictional. Although some information is based on real clients, specific identifying information has been altered extensively. Some of the cases include the following:

- Aaban, a 48-year-old Muslim Iranian immigrant, the son of a violent alcoholic father;
- Juan, a 32-year-old Mexican American who is struggling to maintain a relationship after being raised by a substance-abusing mother;
- Bud, a 44-year-old man who has been laid off from his job and is struggling with a sense of ongoing helplessness after a long and complicated relationship with his heroin-addicted brother;
- Maria, a 12-year-old Puerto Rican American girl who has an alcoholic father and who is caught in a parentified role within her family and a fused relationship with her mother;
- Calvin, an 18-year-old African American man who is struggling to create a meaningful identity as a Jamaican American first-generation college student dealing with issues related to his father's alcoholism; and
- Lakshmi, a 36-year-old advertisement executive who is continuing to enable her alcoholic husband by regularly making excuses for him.

As demonstrated in these brief case descriptions, the diversity of this population of clients is vast. Therefore, it is important to note at the outset that the details shared in this book will not apply to all individuals who have lived with a family member struggling with an SUD. Instead, it is my intention in this book to present the accumulated knowledge of this population. This information, synthesized in this manner, is meant to assist practicing counselors and counselors-in-training as they consider working with individuals who have lived with or currently live with an individual with an SUD. Much of what is presented is designed to help counselors conceptualize cases with individuals who have a history of familial substance abuse or addiction, as considering the impact of this particular experience on a client is often key in understanding patterns and issues that impede psychological well-being. In addition, I provide information regarding the use of specific treatment strategies and techniques. More fully elaborated cases are used throughout the text to provide an opportunity to apply the material presented.

Chapter 1

Substance Abuse and SUD: History and Definition

Issues of substance abuse and addiction are not new. In fact, evidence suggests that humans have been using mind-altering substances since the beginning of time (Segal, 2014). However, national awareness of drug addiction as a potential problem emerged slowly. In the United States, the first drug identified as potentially harmful was opium. In response to an increase in the recreational use of opium in San Francisco, the city invoked the first law associated with drugs when it banned opium dens in 1875. This law eventually led to legislation, passed in 1906, requiring accurate labeling of patent medicines containing opium. Subsequently, in 1914, the Harrison Narcotic Act was passed, prohibiting the sale of large doses of opiates or cocaine, except by licensed physicians. This first step at governmental oversight seemed to have an influence on substance abuse, as the use of narcotics and cocaine decreased. In fact, in this spirit of temperance, the 18th Amendment to the Constitution, which prohibited the use of alcohol, was passed in 1919 and remained in effect until it was repealed in 1933 (Stevens & Smith, 2013).

Upon the repeal of Prohibition in the 1930s, drug education emerged as a concept for the first time, and schools began to incorporate educational programs designed to intervene in adolescent use of drugs and alcohol. However, despite these efforts, drinking and drug use increased. In the 1950s, the use of marijuana, amphetamines, and tranquilizers increased dramatically (Brown, 1981). The 1960s was seen as a time of tremendous social upheaval, and there was a perception of increased drug and alcohol use. However, despite this perception, a 1969 Gallup poll revealed that although 48% of American adults felt that drug use was a serious problem within their communities, only 4% had tried marijuana. It was in the 1970s that marijuana use dramatically increased. By 1973, 12% of American adults reported using marijuana, and by 1977, this percentage had doubled (Robison, 2002a).

By 1985, one third of American adults reported using marijuana, and the use of cocaine was on the rise. It was at this time that crack cocaine was introduced. In a 1986 Gallup poll, when asked what the most serious drug problem was within the United States, adults reported crack cocaine above heroin, marijuana, and alcohol. In response, President Ronald Reagan signed the Anti-Drug Abuse Act of 1986, thus declaring the nation's war on drugs, and Nancy Reagan began the "Just Say No" campaign (Robison, 2002b). The 1986 bill imposed mandatory minimum sentences for the possession of controlled substances in an effort to deter the sale and use of the newly introduced synthetic drugs, including crack cocaine. As funding for this initiative became available, programs began to emerge in response to Reagan's call for action. Perhaps the most widely publicized and used of these was the Drug Abuse Resistance Education (DARE) program, which was introduced in schools across the country. DARE and other programs initiated in the 1980s generally included an educational component designed to teach children about the various substances that were being abused along with activities designed to bolster adolescents' refusal skills.

The 1990s was marked by the first reported decrease in drug use since the 1960s. Although 34% of American reported having used marijuana, the 1999 Gallup youth survey showed a decrease in adolescents' trial use of all controlled substances. However, at the same time, club drugs and methamphetamines (often referred to as crystal meth or meth) began to emerge. During the 1990s, drugs like Ecstasy (a designer club drug) were new and perceived as harmless by adolescents. Given the addictive qualities of methamphetamines, the use of such synthetic drugs began to increase. Finally, in the later 1990s, an increase in the use of heroin was seen, as opiate-based prescription drugs hit the market for the treatment of pain (Robison, 2002b).

The United Nations Office on Drugs and Crime (UNODC) released a report in 2008 outlining the trends in drug usage between the years of 2000 and 2008. During that period, the United States saw a marked increase in the use of illicit drugs from 11% of the adult population in 2000 to 15% in 2008. Specifically, there was a moderate increase in the use of Ecstasy-type and other synthetic drugs and a significant increase in the use of marijuana, hashish, and pain reliev-ers (UNODC, 2008).

Since 2008, the use of heroin has increased; in addition, the face of heroin users has changed over the decades. Whereas the typical heroin user in the 1960s was found to be male and young, with a mean age of 16.5, the heroin addict of today tends to be older, with a mean age of 22.9, and may be male or female. In addition, the use of heroin has moved from predominantly urban areas to the suburbs. Finally, research suggested that the road to heroin use was historically initiated by the use of other increasingly powerful substances. How-ever, 75% of current heroin users report that their use of heroin was initiated by the use of prescription pain medications (Cicero, Ellis, Surratt, & Kurtz, 2014). This trend has been highlighted in current news stories across the country, as the use of heroin continues to rise and spread to communities where it was rarely seen in past decades (Svrluga, 2014).

Defining Substance Abuse and Addiction

In the fifth edition of the *Diagnostic and Statistical Manual* (*DSM-5*; American Psychiatric Association [APA], 2013), substance use disorder (SUD) combines the *DSM-IV* (APA, 2000) categories of substance abuse and substance dependence into a single disorder measured on a continuum from mild to severe. These changes were initiated in response to several concerns and questions raised regarding the criteria described in the *DSM-IV*. To be specific, the work group charged with developing the substance abuse and dependence-related diagnostic criteria for the *DSM-5* conducted extensive research in the form of both literature reviews and empirical studies. Their findings, which were based on analyses of data accumulated from over 200,000 par-ticipants, led to the combining of abuse and dependence criteria into a single SUD. In addition, on the basis of their extensive analyses, the group recommended dropping legal problems and adding craving as criteria and moving gambling disorders to the chapter formerly reserved for substance-related disorders (Hasin et al., 2012).

Ultimately, according to the *DSM-5*, an SUD is described as a pattern of symptoms resulting from use of a substance that the individual continues to take despite the experience of negative con-sequences resulting directly from the substance use. SUD includes the following:

- intoxication;
- substance-induced bipolar and related disorders;
- substance-induced delirium;
- substance-induced depressive disorders, substance-induced anxiety disorders, substance-induced obsessive-compulsive and related disorders;

- substance-induced mental disorders, including substance-induced psychosis;
- substance-induced neurocognitive disorders;
- substance-induced sleep disorders;
- substance-induced sexual dysfunctions; and
- withdrawal.

According the *DSM-5*, SUD spans a wide variety of issues arising from substance use and covers 11 different criteria. An example of Alcohol Use Disorder follows:

A. A problematic pattern of alcohol use leading to clinically significant impairment or distress, as manifested by at least two of the following, occurring within a 12-month period.
1. Alcohol is often taken in larger amounts or over a longer period than was intended.
2. There is a persistent desire or unsuccessful efforts to cut down or control alcohol use.
3. A great deal of time is spent in activities necessary to obtain alcohol, use alcohol, or recover from its effects.
4. Craving, or a strong desire to use alcohol.
5. Recurrent alcohol use resulting in a failure to fulfill major role obligations at work, school, or home.
6. Continued alcohol use despite having persistent or recurrent social or interpersonal problems caused or exacerbated by the effects of alcohol.
7. Important social, occupational, or recreational activities are given up or reduced because of alcohol use.
8. Recurrent alcohol use in situations in which it is physically hazardous.
9. Alcohol use is continued despite knowledge of having a persistent or recurrent physical or psychological problem that is likely to have been caused or exacerbated by alcohol.
10. Tolerance, as defined by either of the following:
    a. A need for markedly increased amounts of alcohol to achieve intoxication or desired effect.
    b. A markedly diminished effect with continued use of the same amount of alcohol.
11. Withdrawal, as manifested by either of the following:
    a. The characteristic withdrawal syndrome for alcohol (refer to Criteria A and B of the criteria set for alcohol withdrawal, pp. 499–500).
    b. Alcohol (or a closely related substance, such as a benzodiazepine) is taken to relieve or avoid withdrawal symptoms.

Note. From the *Diagnostic and Statistical Manual of Mental Disorders,* Fifth Edition (pp. 490–491), by American Psychiatric Association, 2013, Arlington, VA: American Psychiatric Association. Copyright 2013 by American Psychiatric Association. Reprinted with permission. All Rights Reserved.

The *DSM-5* allows clinicians to specify how severe the SUD is, depending on how many symptoms are identified. Two or three symptoms indicate a mild SUD, four or five symptoms indicate a moderate SUD, and six or more symptoms indicate a severe SUD. Clinicians can also add "in early remission," "in sustained remission," "on maintenance therapy," and "in a controlled environment" to the diagnosis.

Although this approach to diagnosis allows for flexibility and a range of disorders that differentiate clients who abuse substances, it does not include criteria indicating when or in what manner the disorder might affect individuals close to the substance abuser. Although a *DSM* diagnosis for this phenomenon (i.e., for codependence) has been suggested, it has never been incorporated into the *DSM* as a distinct disorder. Thus, although there is ample evidence supporting the specific needs of this client population (i.e., individuals affected by another's substance use), no definitive criteria exist for assessing and treating these individuals.

Defining Substance Abuse for the Purposes of This Book

This book is designed to assist professional counselors and counselors-in-training in assessing and treating clients who have a close relationship with a person who has an SUD. Although some of these clients will likely be struggling with their own substance use issues, the target population may not be abusing substances themselves. Instead, they are struggling with the impact of at least one close relationship with an individual who has an SUD. Because an SUD can often go undiagnosed, for the purposes of this book, the client population discussed includes individuals who perceive that the substance use of an individual close to them is affecting their sense of well-being and ability to cope and function at an optimal level. The client may report that the substance use of another is affecting his or her physical, psychological, occupational, or relational well-being.

Chapter 2

Etiological Models of SUD

There are a number of explanatory models of SUD. Among the one-dimensional models are the moral models, the medical models, and the psychodynamic model. In addition, more current multidimensional models have been proposed that explain addiction from multiple perspectives. The most common of the multidimensional models is the biopsychosocial model (Smith & Seymour, 2001; Tombs, 2013).

Moral Models

The moral models of SUD seek to explain addictive behavior as a moral failing. In particular, the "dry" moral model proposes that addiction is simply and only attributable to poor moral choices on the part of the substance abuser. The "wet" moral model, on the other hand, acknowledges that drinking is a normal part of society and may not always be considered an immoral behavior. However, this model suggests that there are implicit rules that govern drinking behavior. Although most adults follow these rules, the individual with an SUD does not and instead chooses to drink in a manner that opposes the normal social order.

Most current-day practitioners do not use moral models as a way of explaining or understanding an SUD. However, there are professionals who retain the belief that addiction can be explained by poor decision making. To be specific, some behavioral models explain the cause of addiction as rooted in behavior; as such, it is under the control of the individual struggling with an SUD. These models do not imply a moral failing on the part of the substance abuser, but they do attribute the disorder to the substance abuser's behavior and choices (Heyman, 2013).

Medical Models

Two medical models have been used to explain addiction—the "old" medical model and the "new" medical model. The old medical model combines the disease concept with the moral model. The initial use of any substance is seen as a choice. However, as the use of the substance increases to the point where a disorder is diagnosed, use is no longer viewed as a choice. At this point, the individual is characterized as having a disease that requires treatment. According to the old medical model, addiction is a fatal, progressive disease that originates with the immoral behavior of excessive drinking.

The new medical model also explains an SUD as a fatal, progressive disease. However, according to this model, the substance abuser possesses a body chemistry or predisposition that promotes addiction. The new medical model describes an SUD as a disease that requires medical attention. There is no reference to any type of moral failing associated with the onset of the disease, and it is fully understood as a medical condition.

The new medical model is widely endorsed, and a medical explanation for SUD has become increasingly credible and mainstream. In fact, it has been argued that the neurobiological changes that occur for the individual with an SUD prove that substance abuse cannot be characterized as a choice for these individuals (Leyton, 2013). The medical models explain the physical attributes associated with addiction and allow for the exploration of medical means of withdrawing from some substances. Exploration of these topics is perhaps the most widely expanding body of research currently available pertaining to the science of SUD. That is, the ever-evolving understanding of what happens within the brain of the individual with an SUD is adding to our understanding of addiction as a medical issue.

For example, from a scientific perspective, an SUD is conceptualized as a cycle of decreased function of brain reward systems. In fact, it has been shown that the reward set point for substance abusers is altered (Koob & Le Moal, 2008). The neurobiological changes in the brain circuitry of an individual with an SUD create a response whereby the substance abuser is neither able to stimulate a sense of reward from continued use of the same amount of a substance nor to experience the antireward responses typical for most individuals (e.g., fear of being arrested). It is hypothesized that it is the rewarding effects of abused drugs that explain why humans use them and laboratory animals self-administer them (Volkow, Wang, Fowler, & Tomasi, 2012). Although the neurobiological processes that underlie vulnerability to substance abuse are still poorly understood, the current study of affected brain function is beginning to unravel some of the medical explanations for drug abuse and addiction. Brain imaging studies suggest that individual variations in several neurotransmitters and in brain circuitry, including circuits involved in reward and motivation, contribute to the explanation of addiction vulnerability (Ersche et al., 2012).

Psychodynamic Model

Psychoanalysts explain SUD in much the same way they describe other psychological disorders. From a psychoanalytic perspective, addiction is viewed as a symptom of underlying neurosis. The psychoanalytic view presumes that the addictive behavior has its roots in early experiences and relationships, and that the behavior itself is a means of expressing unconscious, unresolved conflict.

Although most current-day practitioners will not treat addiction using a purely psychodynamic model, a focus on environmental factors, including those that occurred in early childhood, usually contributes to the overall treatment plan. In fact, at several well-known treatment facilities throughout the country, a psychodynamic approach is endorsed as a piece of an integrated model of treatment. The Caron Foundation, for example, refers to the psychodynamic approach on its website, explaining that addiction can be explained in part by the unconscious processes that result from early experiences. In addition, a clinician might conceptualize relapse as regression to past drug-use behaviors and therefore as symptomatic of an underdeveloped ego (Goodman, n.d.). Even within the medical community, support has been given for the application of a neuropsychoanalytic framework in understanding the complex nature of SUD. This perspective combines the newly acquired medical and biological knowledge with a psychoanalytic view of personality development to provide a framework for creating more effective public health interventions targeting SUD (Johnson, 2013).

Biopsychosocial Model

The biopsychosocial model of addiction includes components of all of the above-mentioned models (with the exception of the moral model). This model provides a comprehensive framework for exploring the interactions and intricacies of SUD. The biopsychosocial model was first introduced by George Engel (1977), and it has since been described and endorsed by other practitioners and researchers (Donovan & Marlatt, 2005; Griffiths, 2005).

The biopsychosocial model of addiction attempts to capture the biological, psychological, and social components of addiction in one explanatory model. It recognizes the complexity of addiction and attempts to explain it as a multidimensional issue that can encompass all of these factors. For example, this model encourages practitioners to assess genetic predisposition, neurochemistry, and the fight-or-flight response from a biological perspective. In addition, psychological attributes such as learning, emotion regulation, stress management, and coping strategies are assessed. And finally, social variables are considered. Level of social support, family background, multicultural considerations, and interpersonal relationships are explored in the context of the SUD. Essentially, within this model, practitioners are able to consider risk factors as well as protective factors in a holistic manner.

Although practitioners continue to differ with regard to the optimal explanatory model of addiction, the most robust and inclusive model is likely the biopsychosocial model. The biopsychosocial model encompasses aspects of the other described models by accounting for the wide variety of factors that affect the development of an SUD. In addition, this model broadly accounts for the biological component of addiction, which is perhaps the most prominently researched area in terms of etiology at this point in time. In fact, the American Society of Addiction Medicine (ASAM) defines addiction with a heavy emphasis on the biological attributes of the condition (ASAM, n.d.). Their definition begins by claiming that addiction is a disease of the brain reward and motivation systems, and it goes on to discuss the role of genetics and brain circuitry. At the same time, the biopsychosocial model recognizes the psychological and social aspects of addiction and addresses these pieces as well. In this way, the biopsychosocial model provides the broadest and most comprehensive means of conceptualizing an SUD.

Chapter 3

Commonly Abused Substances

Keeping up with the variety of substances being abused is difficult, as the profile of drugs and drug-use patterns are constantly changing. However, there are several categories of illicit substances that remain popular among drug abusers. At the current time, the most commonly abused substances fall into the following categories: sedative-hypnotics/depressants, cannabinoids, opioids, stimulants, hallucinogens, inhalants, and synthetic drugs (see Table 1).

Sedative-Hypnotics/Depressants

Sedative-hypnotic drugs work primarily by depressing the central nervous system. These drugs bind to receptors in the central nervous system and inhibit neurotransmitters in the brain. The most popular sedative-hypnotic drug is alcohol. According to the National Institute on Alcohol Abuse and Alcoholism (NIAAA), alcohol continues to be the most widely used mind-altering substance, and it is the drug most likely to be abused (Hinson & Rehm, 2013).

In addition to alcohol, several other depressant drugs are commonly abused. Most of these were originally developed for medical use but eventually became substances that were used recreationally. For example, barbiturates and benzodiazepines were created to alleviate the symptoms associated with anxiety. Although originally thought to be wonder drugs that did not run the risk of dependence

Table 1

Commonly Abused Substances

Category and Drug	Street and Prescription Names	Medical Uses	Addiction Risk
Sedative hypnotics/depressants			
Alcohol	Liquor, beer, wine	None	Moderate
Barbiturates	Phenobarb, reds, yellow jackets, rainbows	Seizure disorders; sleep aid	Various
Benzodiazepines	Xanax, Klonopin, Valium, Ativan, tranks, candy, downers	Relieve anxiety; sleep aid; alcohol and substance withdrawal; muscle relaxant	Various
Cannabinoids			
Marijuana (THC)	Weed, pot, grass, joint, ganja, blunt, herb, Mary Jane, reefer, green, trees	Reduces nausea in cancer patients; treatment of glaucoma	Moderate
Hashish	Hash, hash oil, hemp, boom, gangster	None	Moderate
Opioids			
Heroin	Smack, dope, horse, H, junk	None	High
Opium	Big O, black stuff, block gum, hop	Treatment of diarrhea	High
Oxycodone	Oxy, O.C., oxycotton, percs, Percocet	Pain management	High
Codeine	Captain Cody, Cody, schoolboy	Cough suppression; pain management	High
Stimulants			
Cocaine	Coke, blow, toot, snow, C, crack, rock	Anesthesia: local (ear, nose, throat)	High
Amphetamines	Bennies, black beauties, speed, uppers	ADD; narcolepsy; depression (rare)	High
Methamphetamines	Meth, ice, crank, crystal, fire, speed, Ritalin	Same as amphetamines	High
Hallucinogens			
LSD	Acid, blotter, microdot	None	Low
Mescaline	Mesc, peyote, buttons	None	Low
Psilocybin	Magic mushrooms, shrooms, purple passion	None	Low
MDA; MDMA	Ecstasy	None	Low
PCP	Angel dust, hog	Veterinary anesthetic	Low

(Continued)

Table 1 (*Continued*)
Commonly Abused Substances

Category and Drug	Street and Prescription Names	Medical Uses	Addiction Risk
Inhalants			
Commercial solvents	Paint, paint thinner, gasoline, glue	None	Moderate
Gases	Aerosol nitrous oxide, laughing gas, whippets	Nitrous oxide is used for anesthesia	Unknown
Nitrites	Poppers, snappers	None	Unknown
Synthetic drugs			
MDMA	Ecstasy	None	Unknown
Synthetic cannabinoids	Cloud 9, mojo	None	Unknown

Note. Various = addiction risk range varies depending on drug; THC = tetrahydrocannabinol; ADD = attention-deficit disorder; LSD = lysergic acid diethylamide; MDA and MDMA = methylenedioxyamphetamine.

or harsh side effects, it was not long before the medical and addictions communities became aware of the increase in barbiturate and benzodiazepine abuse. One of the primary issues associated with sedative-hypnotic/depressant use is tolerance. Over time, the body adjusts to the drug and it no longer has the desired effect; thus, there is a need for increased dosage. This increased dosage also creates a physical dependence, which leads to severe withdrawal symptoms for an individual who attempts to stop taking the drug.

Alcohol

As mentioned in the previous section, the most commonly abused mind-altering substance is alcohol (NIAAA, n.d.). From the time of cave dwellers, there are accounts of alcohol use and abuse (Smith & Seymour, 2001). Aside from its addictive nature, alcohol on its own can cause enormous damage to physical, psychological, relational, and emotional health. In fact, more substance-related deaths occur nationwide as the result of alcohol use than from all other psychoactive substances combined. In addition, the economic impact of alcohol use and abuse is enormous, and alcohol is frequently reported as the first mind-altering substance used by people who eventually develop an SUD.

Perhaps one of the most insidious aspects of alcohol use is the fact that it is so readily available and so socially acceptable. It is used recreationally in numerous settings and contexts; in fact, it is a part of virtually every social event. It is extremely difficult for any adult to completely avoid contact with alcohol. In addition, because most children grow up seeing alcohol as a robust and central component of the adult lifestyle, they, too, are vulnerable to the pervasive impact of alcohol.

Alcohol is a central nervous system depressant. As such, it lowers neurotransmission levels within the brain and lowers stimulation. When ingested in large quantities, intoxication ensues; the results are a decrease in mental and physical acuity, an unsteady gait, slurred speech, slowed reactions, and mechanical difficulties. As alcohol intake increases, so do the long-term health risks that accompany this drug. Some of the risks include an increased likelihood of the following: injury, violence, fetal damage in pregnant women, depression, neurological deficits, hypertension, liver and heart disease, and fatal overdose. Despite these risks, alcohol use disorder continues to plague between 8% and 10% of the population (NIAAA, n.d.).

Barbiturates

Barbiturates were originally developed as a sleep aid and to treat anxiety. However, when the addictive quality of barbiturates was recognized, prescriptions began to decline in number. Currently used primarily in the treatment of seizure disorders and muscle tension, these drugs are not as available as they once were. This decline in availability is primarily the result of the introduction of benzodiazepines. Benzodiazepines are the current drug of choice for treating anxiety, as they are thought to have fewer side effects and to be less addictive than the traditionally prescribed barbiturates.

Benzodiazepines

Among the most commonly prescribed drugs, benzodiazepines were developed as a safer option with less potential for abuse than barbiturates. There are currently 15 varieties of benzodiazepines on the market, all of which have been approved by the Food and Drug Administration (FDA; WebMD, n.d.). Used primarily in the treatment of anxiety, benzodiazepines work to increase a specific neurotransmitter chemical within the brain thought to reduce brain activity. Although these drugs are effective in the treatment of anxiety, there has been a marked increase in the recreational use of benzodiazepines (Jones, Mogali, & Comer, 2012). In fact, the number of deaths attributed to benzodiazepines was 5 times higher in 2009 than it was a decade prior, and emergency room visits related to the abuse of benzodiazepines increased 89% throughout that same decade (Jann, Kennedy, & Lopez, 2014; National Institute on Drug Abuse [NIDA], 2014b).

Cannabinoids

Cannabinoids include both marijuana and hashish. Marijuana is derived from the cannabis plant and is intended for use as a psychoactive substance. It is generally smoked, although it is also occasionally swallowed (i.e., cooked into edibles), and its effects include euphoria, elevated mood, and relaxation. Hashish is composed of compressed cannabis. It contains the same active ingredient as marijuana, tetrahydrocannabinol (THC), but in higher concentrations. Used recreationally, hashish is generally smoked.

Despite being a commonly used recreational drug, cannabinoids can cause health problems, including impairment in one's ability to learn, decline in mental health, negative respiratory effects (including frequent infections), possible reproductive problems (including low birth weight), and possible impaired immune functioning. Yet, more states are legalizing marijuana, and the medical use of cannabinoids has increased. That is, marijuana is used to reduce nausea and stimulate the appetite for cancer patients as well as to treat glaucoma. In addition, research is currently underway to assess the use of cannabinoids to treat cardiovascular disease (Durst & Lotan, 2011).

There is disagreement regarding the addictive qualities of cannabinoids, but the National Institute on Drug Abuse (NIDA) does list cannabinoids as addictive, largely because of the rising potency of the cannabinoids currently being sold (NIDA, n.d.). Although tolerance to these drugs does not seem to increase as it does with most addictive substances, individuals report use patterns indicative of addictive behavior. There are numerous reported cases of individuals using cannabis daily for extended periods of time. In addition, marijuana is clearly a gateway drug. Virtually all individuals with an SUD report initially using marijuana or hash prior to using more addictive and potentially dangerous substances.

Opioids

Opioids, derived from the poppy plant, bond to opioid receptors found primarily in the nervous system. Useful in pain management, opioids decrease the sensation of pain and increase tolerance for pain. Opioids occur as both natural and synthetic substances. For example, morphine is the substance contained in the resin of the opium poppy, whereas oxycodone represents a partially synthetic opioid.

Abuse of opioids has occurred throughout history. The most commonly abused opiate is currently heroin. Converted into morphine in the body, heroin is known for creating an overwhelming sense of euphoria. Tolerance for heroin develops quickly, creating a need for an increase in dosage to elicit the desired effects. In addition, addiction occurs quickly because of the drug's impact on the central nervous system.

In addition to heroin, a more current phenomenon of addiction to opiate-based prescription pain medication has emerged. Prescription pain medications (e.g., OxyContin, Vicodin, Percocet) are generally crushed and snorted into the nose as a way of inducing the same euphoric effect produced by heroin use. As the legitimate use of prescription pain medications has skyrocketed, the abuse of these drugs has risen as well. It is estimated that in 1991, approximately 76 million prescriptions were written for oxycodone. By 2013, 207 million such prescriptions were written, coinciding with a dramatic increase in the abuse of this drug. As a result, drug companies have begun to create addictive-resistant forms of prescription pain medication, and pharmacies have made the sale and distribution of these drugs more controlled. These changes seem to have had an effect on the rate of abuse of prescription pain medications. However, although the abuse of these medications seems to be declining slightly, deaths associated with the abuse of prescription pain medications increased by 300% between 2001 and 2013 (NIDA, 2014a).

In addition, the recent decline in the abuse of prescription pain medications has been accompanied by an increase in the use of heroin by a different demographic than has been seen in the past. Instead of the inner-city face one has come to associate with the abuse of heroin, current use patterns have shifted, and the new demographic includes more affluent, White individuals (Cicero et al., 2014). The number of heroin addicts is predicted to have doubled between 2005 and 2012, and this increase has occurred predominantly among White adolescents and young adults (NIDA, 2014b). This phenomenon is thought to be partially the result of the increased level of difficulty obtaining prescription pain medications and the prohibitive cost of these drugs. In addition, younger heroin addicts are beginning their use by smoking the drug, perhaps believing that this will mediate the addictive qualities of heroin. This belief is false, though, and the number of adolescents and young adults addicted to heroin is on the rise. In addition, many of these people addicted to heroin are likely to evolve to using heroin intravenously, because such use is reported to produce the most intense rush as compared with smoking or snorting the drug. Injecting also produces the least waste of the drug and introduces the drug rapidly into the blood stream.

Discontinuation of opioids is associated with serious and severe withdrawal symptoms. Opioids are both psychologically and physically addictive; therefore, a person addicted to them can suffer serious, sometimes life-threatening effects in attempting to withdraw from opiate-based substances. Thus, hospitalization is highly recommended during the detoxification period.

Stimulants

As a class of drugs, stimulants are known for inducing a temporary state of perceived improvement in mental or physical functioning. The effects of stimulants on the central nervous system result in increased wakefulness, alertness, endurance, and productivity. In addition, stimulants often improve mood and can reduce anxiety. Like other classes of drugs, stimulants have legitimate medical uses but also have some potential side effects. Some of these side effects include weight loss, insomnia, cardiac and cardiovascular complications, strokes, and seizures. Drugs within this class are ingested through snorting, smoking, injecting, and swallowing. The illicit use of stimulants occurs most often in the form of cocaine, amphetamine, and methamphetamine abuse.

Amphetamines

Amphetamines are often referred to as *speed*. Commonly associated with dieting and losing weight, these drugs were initially introduced to suppress appetite. However, amphetamine abuse is not uncommon, and such abuse is currently on the rise given the introduction of methamphetamine.

Cocaine

Cocaine, derived from the coca leaf, is a central nervous system stimulant. As such, it stimulates the brain. It is addictive because of its effect on the limbic system. That is, cocaine enhances the limbic reward pathway, creating a sense of well-being. Cocaine is often abused in powder form. It can be snorted into the nose or injected.

In the 1980s, a new form of cocaine emerged: crack. Crack is a form of cocaine that has been processed to create a rock crystal. Crack cocaine is generally smoked and is extremely addictive. In fact, drug abusers often report addiction to crack cocaine after only one use. The processing of cocaine into crack produced a drug that was far less expensive and so is available to a wider range of individuals. However, the effects of crack cocaine are not as long-lasting as the powdered form of cocaine; thus, the user needs to obtain more of the drug on a more consistent basis once an addiction has taken hold (NIDA, 2013).

Methamphetamines

Methamphetamine (i.e., *crystal meth*) is a neurotoxin originally produced to treat attention-deficit/hyperactivity disorder (ADHD). Although prescription methamphetamine abuse has increased, the most commonly abused form of this drug is crystal meth. Crystal meth is generally manufactured in makeshift labs using relatively inexpensive and easily accessible products as well as highly toxic substances. Methamphetamines are often smoked, releasing a rush of dopamine to the brain, which creates an intense surge of pleasure and a feeling of euphoria. However, it can also be ingested orally, snorted, or injected intravenously. Crystal meth is highly addictive and damages the central nervous system, eventually changing the molecular structure of the brain (NIDA, 2014c).

Hallucinogens

Unlike the other categories of drugs discussed thus far, hallucinogens have been historically known for their role in religion and ceremonies among a variety of groups. Today, most of the drugs in this class are synthetically manufactured. However, hallucinogens were traditionally found in nature. The most popular and commonly abused hallucinogen is lysergic acid diethylamide (LSD). Despite LSD being a newer drug discovered in the 1940s, its main component, ergotamine, has a much longer history. Originally used as an ingredient in mystic potions associated with spiritual ceremonies, ergotamine was used in the 19th century as a potential treatment for psychotic symptoms and to treat alcoholism and other addictions.

At the current time, hallucinogens are primarily used recreationally, and the most commonly available hallucinogens are LSD, Ecstasy-type drugs, and mushrooms. They are generally ingested through smoking or swallowing or are absorbed through tissue in the mouth (NIDA, 2009). Use of hallucinogens results in the attainment of altered states of perception and feelings, along with hallucinations. Several of these drugs also increase body temperature, heart rate, and blood pressure to dangerous levels. Although hallucinogens are not thought to be addictive, they carry such potential side effects as flashbacks to drug-induced incidents long after using, depression, psychosis, nausea, paranoia, panic, and impulsive behavior.

Inhalants

Inhalants are a class of drugs easily accessed. Because of the ease in obtaining these substances, children and adolescents commonly begin a pattern of destructive drug use with inhalants. In fact, inhalants are the only substances that are used and abused more by younger teens than by older adolescents or adults (NIDA, 2012b). Generally used by breathing in the substance through the nose or mouth, the gases released—primarily nitrates—create a short-term high. Use of inhalants is commonly referred to as *sniffing* or *huffing*, and many common household items can be abused. For example, glue, markers, and aerosol sprays can be inhaled to create a sense of euphoria. Depending on the substance used, a variety of dangerous side effects can ensue. Neurological and major organ damage has been attributed to the use of inhalants (NIDA, 2012b).

Synthetic Drugs

Most recently, the use of synthetic drugs has emerged as one of the most overwhelming and frightening issues for individuals attempting to control and understand drug-use patterns and recovery implications. Beginning with Ecstasy, synthetic (i.e., designer) drugs have become a significant force within the substance abuse world. Synthetic drugs are precisely what the name suggests: These are drugs that are synthetically developed in laboratories. As opposed to the substances that have come from plants or natural processes (fermentation), synthetic drugs are manufactured for the express purpose of potential abuse. Oftentimes, these substances are created using a variety of commonly known household products or over-the-counter medications. The developers of synthetic drugs have discovered ways to adjust the chemical composition of a variety of commonly known substances in such a way that they can create products used to alter an individual's state of consciousness.

The most frightening aspect of this newfound endeavor is that new drugs are being developed on an ongoing basis and at a staggeringly swift pace. In addition, the developers of these substances are able to use products and chemicals that are legal and readily available. For example, in 2014, an Ohio high school senior lost his life to powdered caffeine. In this case, adolescents and young adults found that they could purchase caffeine powder online. Believing that they were simply ingesting something that is commonplace and is found in many of the beverages they consume, these students decided that ingesting this powdered caffeine would be a relatively safe way to gain the stimulating benefits of caffeine. In another example, synthetic cannabinoids have emerged as a new phenomenon. Often referred to as *cloud 9* or *mojo*, these drugs are chemically similar to marijuana. Again, the allure of a synthetic substance that is perceived to be as safe as marijuana has drawn adolescents to try this drug. However, the new compounds used to create synthetic cannabinoids have resulted in numerous hospitalizations, overdoses, and aggressive and suicidal behavior. Most recently, a warning was issued regarding a new drug known as superman. This particular drug is sold as Ecstasy, but has been shown to contain a lethal dose of a substance not associated with the original forms of Ecstasy (NIDA, 2015).

Keeping up with the developing, manufacturing, and selling of synthetic drugs has posed a new and overwhelming issue for both the law enforcement community and treatment providers. In addition, because these drugs are the products of laboratories and individuals operating with no external controls, it is impossible to know what is being ingested. And yet, despite the warnings and staggering statistics regarding the increased use of synthetic drugs, such drugs continue to flood the market and evolve at an alarming rate.

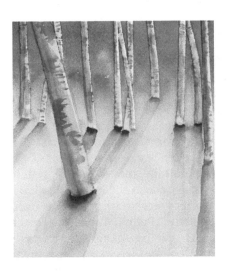

Chapter 4

Family Theory

Counselors who work with the family members of substance abusers should understand some of the theoretical underpinnings of family therapy. This chapter provides an overview and describes some of the specific theories of family therapy. This information is synthesized with attributes that have been shown to be characteristic in families with a substance-abusing member. In addition, this chapter highlights how clinicians can use this theoretical grounding to work with clients who have experienced familial substance abuse. Finally, a case example provides an opportunity to apply the theoretical to practice.

So, how do families tend to operate as systems in a broad sense? It has been suggested that one of the organizing foundations within all families is that of maintaining equilibrium (Hecker, 2014). Family therapists believe that all families will strive for equilibrium. *Equilibrium* is defined as "a state of balance due to the equal action of opposing forces" (Equilibrium, n.d.), and family theory is built upon an assumed understanding that all families strive for this balance. Within a family, equilibrium is established as a way to manage the typical developmental needs of the individual family members, the vast activities of daily living that consume all families, and all of the other challenges that exist for the family within the context of its survival as a system embedded within layers of larger systems. Families will naturally strive to achieve a balance between these factors that push on it and on the resources the family has to deal with these forces. At the same time, the family as a system will work toward a way to meet both the needs of the family as a unit and the needs of its individual members.

When equilibrium is established, families are said to be functioning in a state of homeostasis. Homeostasis represents continuity within the family. It is developed on the basis of family norms that include feedback loops whereby individual family members learn to respond and react in predictable ways that maintain the family's homeostasis (Gladding, 2014). Families will strive to achieve homeostasis regardless of any dysfunction that exists within the system. In fact, if dysfunction has become a norm for the family, homeostasis will incorporate and support that dysfunction. Because homeostasis represents the most comfortable state for a family, members will generally do whatever it takes to maintain this balance in the face of challenges and in response to individual family members' developmental needs. As professional counselors, we understand that change is difficult. In families, the difficulties associated with making changes are exacerbated, as it involves more than one individual and simultaneously involves changing the norms connected to homeostasis for the system.

Oftentimes a change within a family system is initiated by a single member of the family and is not a welcomed challenge for other family members. When one individual within a family decides to change, this change is likely to upset the homeostasis within the system. The predictable response to this disruption is that other members within the family will work very hard to get back to whatever state of homeostasis has become comfortable for that system. In the case of a family that has a member with an SUD, the homeostasis that is achieved is likely to involve enabling the substance-abusing family member. Therefore, when any single member of that family initiates a change, the typical response of the other family members will be to push back in order to maintain the accepted homeostatic state for that system.

For example, if the individual with the SUD is a parent in the system and the other parent decides that he or she would like things to change, the substance abuser is likely to do whatever it takes to maintain homeostasis and fight the change. In fact, it is also likely that other family members will attempt to thwart the change, as they have become comfortable with the homeostasis that has been established. This resistance will make changing significantly more difficult for the sober parent and may result in that parent deciding that it is easier, and perhaps even safer, to forego the change in favor of maintaining homeostasis.

Another example might include a client who has a sibling who is abusing drugs. Perhaps this individual has come to counseling to learn about the possibility of using an intervention with his or her sibling. In exploring this option, the counselor might want to ascertain the feelings of other family members regarding the imposition of an intervention. It is not atypical for other family members to oppose this kind of direct confrontation of the substance abuse issue. Again, this is an example of the power of homeostasis within family systems.

At an increasingly complex level, change within a family also challenges its state of morphostasis. *Morphostasis* in a family refers to the extent to which it can keep its shape. There is a constant tension in families between stability and flexibility. Families need to be stable and predictable in order for the members to carry out activities of daily living, and they must also simultaneously be adaptable and able to change over time in response to the typical developmental stages; in response to crisis, a move, a loss; or in order to disrupt a dysfunctional pattern (Steinglass, 1987). The state of morphostasis reached by any given family exists on a continuum ranging from families with virtually no structure and therefore no discernible shape to families with a rigid structure that does not adapt well to changes. In the case of a family with a substance-abusing member, it is often the case that they will fall at either extreme along this continuum. For such a family, a comfortable state of morphostasis that accommodates the issue of SUD must be reached. This process will require an organizational structure that includes the denial of this specific reality. Thus, these families must avoid connection and genuine interaction and function as separate individuals who happen to be in the same family. Or they must construct a rigid structure that includes rules, roles, and expectations that support the inclusion of the individual who has the SUD.

The systemic tendencies of homeostasis and morphostasis provide the framework for family rules, expectations, roles, and power dynamics. They act as a template used to face activities of daily living and process issues or challenges that inevitably arise over the course of family life. In a family with a substance-abusing member, these structures are likely to support routines that do not necessarily meet the needs of the individual family members in healthy ways. Such families are likely to make the SUD the centerpiece of their family structure.

Most helping professionals conceptualize addiction and SUD within the context of the family. Although much of the work we do as professional counselors is based on theoretical models that target individual growth and development, we will have a deeper understanding of the issues if we use a systems framework as a means of working with individuals who are residing in a system with a substance-abusing member. In fact, it is uncommon practice in the treatment of substance abuse and addictions not to include a family component.

Theories of Family Therapy

There are a number of theoretical frameworks for explaining family functioning (see Table 2). The types of family therapy include psychoanalytic, experiential, Bowenian, structural, and strategic. These theories differ in a number of ways, including where they see the "problem" residing within a family. Psychoanalytic and experiential

Table 2
Theories of Family Therapy

Theory and Theorist	Main Points of the Theory
Psychoanalytic family therapy Freud	• Focus on the unconscious and defense mechanisms • Psychoanalytic theory focuses on the individual • Object relations theory focuses on the family • Examines attachment in young children and the formation of relationships
Experiential family therapy Whitaker, Satir	• Focus on counselor–client/family relationships • Helps clients self-reflect on their relationships with others • Looks at both individual members and the family as a system • Includes family sculpting

Bowenian family therapy
Bowen
	• Focus on family relationships
	• Examines the following:
	    Differentiation of self
	    Triangles
	    Nuclear family emotional process
	    Family projection process
	    Multigenerational transmission process
	    Sibling position
	    Emotional cutoff
	    Societal emotional process

Structural family therapy Minuchin	• Examines family as a system • Therapist joins the family • Creates maps or diagrams to analyze structures within the family
Strategic family therapy Madanes, Haley and Richeport-Haley	• Most directive approach • Identify goals and strategies to meet goals • Therapist maintains a directive role • Focus on addressing specific, identified issues

theories tend toward explaining family functioning as a result of the mental health of the individual family members. Bowenian theory considers the health and history of the individual family members within a systems framework. Structural and strategic theories assert that family issues reside within the system and thus must be addressed at that level (Hecker, 2014).

Psychoanalytic Family Therapy

At the heart of psychoanalytic theory are the role of the unconscious and the use of defense mechanisms to cope with anxiety. According to

Freud, human behavior is motivated primarily from the unconscious mind, and most behavior is motivated by impulses that are outside of conscious awareness (Corey, 2013). From a psychoanalytic perspective, these unconscious mechanisms are formed very early on in the life of an individual through the presumably profound impact of the earliest relationships established.

Object relations theory is the concept within psychoanalytic theory that bridges individual work to family work. In essence, object relations theory asserts that very early relationships result in the formation of mental objects that help us organize how we relate to others. From a psychoanalytic perspective, the manner in which we organize this very important aspect of life (i.e., how we learn to see ourselves in relationships with others) is deeply embedded and forms the basis for how we operate within relationships for the remainder of our lives. Closely associated with attachment theory, the psychoanalytic view of relationships focuses on the need for a secure attachment within our first primary relationship. On the basis of a series of studies, Bowlby (2004) concluded that infants require an attachment to a single, constant figure. If that attachment is characterized as anxious or frustrated, the child is likely to become avoidant or enmeshed. Stack Sullivan (Evens, 2006) suggested that if the attachment were healthy (i.e., not anxious), the child would see himself or herself as good and worthy. However, if the primary caregiver is unable to develop a secure attachment with the infant, the infant will develop a style of relating where that infant sees himself or herself as "bad" or, in the most traumatic cases, will be entirely unable to attach.

From a psychoanalytical perspective, the focus of clinical work is generally targeted at working with individuals. In working with families from this theoretical perspective, clinicians might seek to discover family myths that are created when individuals subconsciously relate to each other. For example, individual family members who have issues that are related to early attachment experiences will often distort or simplify reality. In addition, such families will often work hard to protect themselves from facing unpleasant truths that might be perceived as threatening and will unify around preventing outsiders from learning of realities that might interrupt the organization of the family's emotional life around the myths it has created.

In the case of dysfunctional family systems, the development of both the mental object and a secure attachment is likely to be negatively affected (Jordan & Shaw, 2008). If the primary caregiver within a family is struggling with an SUD, the development of the internalized object for any child in that family will be affected. Because this process is thought to operate outside of conscious awareness, the developing individual will likely learn to perceive the world, and any subsequent relationships, according to the internalized object projected by the substance-abusing parent. A primary caregiver who is struggling with an SUD presumably will be distracted and emotionally unavailable or, at the very least, inconsistent in caring for the developing child. In this case, the child is likely to internalize a presumption that this is representative of the world; thus, the child may be vulnerable to a number of obstacles throughout the developmental process.

Two other constructs at the heart of psychoanalytic theory are separation and individuation. Theoretically, children begin the process of separation very early in life and continue to separate throughout childhood and adolescence. The ultimate goal of raising children in healthy families is to facilitate their growth into healthy, functioning adults who can live independently and contribute to society. It is a paradox that the more a child is loved and nurtured, the easier it is for that child to separate and begin an adult life. Likewise, separating from a dysfunctional family system is far more difficult than separating from a healthy family. For children who grow up in families with a substance abuse issue, the task of separating can be tremendously challenging (Celani, 2005).

There are many iterations of how psychoanalytic family therapy might be applied to working with clients who have lived with a family member struggling with an SUD. To begin with, the counselor will likely assume that the client's family was dysfunctional, and that equilibrium within that family was established to support the substance abuse in the family. The psychoanalytic view would then lead the counselor to assume that the internalized object the client uses to measure and assess the world might be causing issues, especially in the context of relationships. It would also be presumed that the client has not explored or resolved this mechanism and is operating primarily on an unconscious level. Therefore, the client may present with a history of failed relationships or with a history of being attracted to abusive individuals who are unable to meet the client's needs. What the client will be unaware of is that this pattern is most likely the result of the unresolved negative internalized object, and that this pattern is likely linked to the SUD within the family. The psychoanalytically based counselor in this case will likely want to explore the origin of these dynamics and work toward changing the behavior patterns that emerged as a result of the client's very earliest experiences with relationships.

Experiential Family Therapy

Carl Whitaker (1982) and Virginia Satir (1994) are credited with the development of experiential family therapy. As the name suggests, experiential therapy extends beyond traditional talk therapy. Although experiential family therapy is not necessarily recognized as a coherent theoretical model for conducting therapy, it became popular in the 1970s and 1980s. The focus of experiential family therapy is on the counselor–client (i.e., counselor–family) relationship, and a primary goal is to facilitate client exploration of the self in relation to others; in particular, the self in relation to the family. Thus, the emphasis is predominantly on the individual family members but involves the exploration of how they interact as a unique unit.

In the 1980s, the technique of family sculpting evolved as a way for families to act out feelings (Hearn & Lawrence, 1985). This technique involves individual family members arranging their family deliberately so as to depict their individual experience of being a part of that system. Addictions counselors adopted this technique, which allows families and counselors to gain an understanding of how each member views his or her experience of being a part of that system. In using this technique, the counselor asks an individual family member to arrange the family in a way that represents how he or she experiences the system. An example might be asking an adolescent to "sculpt" the family. Perhaps this adolescent feels isolated within the family and also feels that the mother is unavailable. The adolescent might put the rest of the family members together, indicating that they are connected. Perhaps the mother would be completely absent from the scene, and the adolescent would be removed from the rest of the family, possibly turned away from the family. Sculpting allows family members to use an experiential means of expressing their feelings. In this example, the adolescent might be able to describe why he or she sculpted the family in the chosen manner, even if that adolescent has been unable to articulate his or her feelings.

The experiential family therapist is likely to work initially on the development of a trusting and cohesive therapeutic relationship with the client. Again, the presumption can be made that the client's presenting problem will likely involve difficulty with relationships. Therefore, the experiential therapist will conceptualize the counselor–client relationship as the primary vehicle for healing. Assuming that the client has a history of familial substance abuse, the counselor will work to assist the client in exploring his or her experience of being a part of that family. The counselor will seek to understand the covert messages and understandings that the client may have obtained within the family. In order to facilitate this process, the counselor may use a family sculpting technique. Assuming the family is not present in the session, the counselor may ask the client to arrange figures according to how he or she feels in the family. For example, the client might report a particularly disturbing episode involving his or her parents and two siblings. The counselor might suggest that the client enact the episode or draw the episode, placing people in positions symbolic of the client's experience. Perhaps the client felt invisible during the episode and therefore might place himself or herself in a position where nobody else can see him or her. Or the client might express awareness of the younger siblings' fear and their desire for the episode to stop. In this case, the client might portray the siblings covering their ears or may put himself or herself between the younger siblings and the parents. The ultimate goal of counseling from an experiential point of view is to assist the client in articulating and sharing the experience of growing up with a substance-abusing family member.

Bowenian Family Therapy

Murray Bowen (1978) is credited with developing a theoretical framework for understanding the emotional life of a family. Bowenian therapy is organized around the concept of differentiation (Titelman, 2014). With a focus on how well family members are able to interact as individual selves with healthy boundaries, Bowen's theory is organized around eight interconnected concepts that explain family functioning.

Differentiation of Self

Often described as the cornerstone of Bowen's theory, *differentiation of self* refers to the extent to which individual family members are able to individuate and develop a separate sense of self. Bowenian family therapists believe that in the context of human development, the level of differentiation afforded a child is paramount to the healthy development of that child. In addition, Bowen believed that it is the parents' levels of differentiation that will determine this aspect of development for their children. Bowen asserted that differentiation involves a complicated and multilayered experience within a family, and that it is essential for parents to work toward their own increased levels of differentiation and support the same in their children. Working toward higher levels of differentiation when one has been raised in a dysfunctional system characterized by a lack of differentiation is considered a difficult task involving work on separating from one's family of origin while simultaneously remaining connected. The seven remaining organizing concepts of Bowenian family therapy represent the ways in which families are likely to manage the levels of differentiation they have adopted.

Triangles

Triangles occur within a family when one person within the system is experiencing dissatisfaction with another. Instead of addressing the concerns in a direct manner, the distressed individual invites a third party into the relationship. Although a triangle within a family may serve as means of releasing tension or emotional intensity, it will not assist in solving the underlying issue that has led to its development.

Nuclear Family Emotional Process

From a Bowenian perspective, emotional processes operate over years and develop into recurring, often predictable patterns. The patterns that are formed oftentimes evolve into rules that concern the level of differentiation permitted within the family.

Family Projection Process

Family projection process refers to the ways in which parents transmit their level of differentiation to their children. Healthy, well-differentiated parents are able to be separate enough from their children to allow them to develop an individuated sense of self. In this case, parents are connected to their children and preserve a loving and caring relationship in which they allow their children to become separate and unique individuals who are expected to face and manage the consequences of their behavior. For parents who are not well differentiated, the tendency is toward a distant, disconnected relationship or toward an enmeshed or fused relationship in which the child is not seen as a whole and separate individual.

Multigenerational Transmission Process

Multigenerational transmission process refers to the transmission of the family emotional process through multiple generations. What Bowen has proposed is that the emotional forces that take hold within families are passed through generations and do not reside solely within the current family.

Sibling Position

Incorporating the research of Walter Toman (1998), Bowen has suggested that sibling position affects development within the family. Essentially, Toman's research suggests that individuals who grow up in the same sibling position are likely to share certain characteristics.

Emotional Cutoff

Emotional cutoff is a method of managing undifferentiation, whereby the greater the fusion between generations within a family, the greater the likelihood of emotional cutoff. *Emotional cutoff* refers to the emotional severing of ties within a family. Individuals will attempt to disengage from the family experience. However, according to Bowen, this solution is ineffective, as individuals will tend to reenact the emotional intensity that they have been avoiding in current and future relationships.

Societal Emotional Process

Societal emotional process refers to the emotional processes in society that affect the functioning of families. Bowen suggested that a prolonged exposure to social anxiety leads to a lowering of healthy functioning and differentiation within families. Sexism, racism, and poverty are all examples of social conditions that are likely to affect the functioning of individual families.

The Bowenian family therapist is going to be primarily concerned with assessing the level of differentiation for a client. In the case where the client has lived or is currently living in a family with a substance-abusing member, the assumption might be made that the client is not well differentiated and may be struggling with relationships as a result. In a family where members are encouraged to keep a secret (e.g., the SUD of another family member), it is difficult to differentiate. Aside from the other issues that may plague such a family and discourage differentiation, keeping a secret imposes a mandate on the individual family members that does not allow for a unique or individually developed reaction to the substance abuse within the family.

One of the underlying presumptions addressed within Bowenian theory is that individuals are attracted to and also attract other individuals at about the same level of differentiation as themselves. When an individual has lived in a family where differentiation of self was not supported, that person is far more likely to seek out relationships in which he or she can exist at a level of differentiation comparable to what has become comfortable. In addition, if a client has grown up in a family where triangulated relationships existed to diffuse tension within individual relationships, that client will be easily drawn into triangles as he or she attempts to form relationships outside of the family. That is, the client may feel compelled to agree with a friend or a partner, even when the client does not necessarily view a situation in the same way.

The Bowenian counselor might also look at the various patterns that were established in the family as a way of managing the SUD. The client can be encouraged to critically assess these patterns and challenge those that are unhealthy. There might also be a focus on the multigenerational nature of substance abuse within the family as well as on the social or cultural issues that may have affected family functioning. However, all of these topics will or will not be addressed in the service of expanding the level of differentiation for the client.

Structural Family Therapy

Another theory to explain and describe family functioning is structural theory, which was developed by Salvador Minuchin (1974). According to Minuchin, family issues are not attributable to individuals but instead reside within the system. Therefore, a systems approach is required to resolve family problems.

Structural family therapy begins with the therapist "joining" with the family. In essence, the therapist will work toward becoming a member of the family system in order to begin authentically identifying dysfunctional patterns. Similar to the counselor's initial focus on building rapport within the counselor–client relationship, this process requires the establishment of high levels of trust between the therapist and all of the members of the family system.

Once the therapist has joined the family, the goal is to map or diagram the structure of the family. This process includes mapping both the overt family structures as well as more covert alliances or structures that operate within the system. For example, although the overt family structure may include the subsystems of the two parents and the four biological children, less obvious subsystems could include subsystems of a mother and daughter (if perhaps the mother confides in the daughter as a peer) or a gender subsystem (if males and females are viewed as distinct and perhaps behave and are treated differently within the family). Not all of these subsystems will be inherently dysfunctional. Therefore, it is the job of the therapist to determine the dysfunctional alliances and subsystems, join them, and attempt to disrupt the unhealthy dynamics and restore balanced functioning.

As mentioned above, the structural family therapist begins the counseling process by joining with the client. The concept of joining implies trust building and the use of empathy to reach a deep and solid understanding of the client. From a structural perspective, the work of counseling cannot proceed until the counselor and the client are joined. This process might be affected by familial substance abuse, as trust may be more difficult to elicit if the client has had inconsistent experiences with attachments and important relationships in the past (Minuchin, 2006).

Once joining has been achieved, the structural therapist will maintain a primary focus on boundaries. The focus may be on the client's current family, or it may be on a client's family of origin. From a structural perspective, healthy boundaries are the hallmark of well-functioning families. In the case of a client who has come for counseling because of a current situation with a substance-abusing family member, the therapist will likely focus on the structure of this present-day family. Perhaps a wife has come for counseling because her husband has an alcohol use disorder (AUD). The structural therapist is likely to conceptualize the case using a genogram to illuminate the current subsystems within the family. In this case, the parental subsystem is likely to be dysfunctional, and the counselor might work with the wife to explore the possibilities for restructuring the family. One possibility is to help the wife set a boundary with her husband whereby she will agree to stay in the marriage only if he receives treatment for his AUD. In this case, the counselor may be seeking to strengthen or regain a parental subsystem.

In another case, perhaps a young adult is finding it difficult to engage in healthy relationships. Assuming that this client grew up in a home with a substance-abusing family member, the structural family therapist might want to explore the structure of this client's family of origin. This work might include uncovering some of the dysfunction in the family of origin by looking at the various subsystems that existed and gaining an understanding of how and why they might have become the norm for that family. In doing this work, clients can begin to conceptualize their current issues as they relate to the kinds of boundaries that have become normal for them. Perhaps these boundaries and structures worked well as a survival mechanism in the client's family of origin. However, they may not be effective in the development of healthy adult relationships.

Strategic Family Therapy

Strategic family therapy is perhaps the most directive of the family therapy approaches. Jay Haley and Madeleine Richeport-Haley (2007) and Cloe Madanes (1981) are credited with developing strategic family therapy as a means of addressing family issues directly, with precise intent. Within this theoretical framework, family goals are identified and specific strategies are developed to meet those goals. These strategies might involve changes that individual family members are assigned to make, or they may involve systemwide changes that are initiated by the therapist. The therapist is expected to maintain a directive role within the therapeutic process, and seeks to identify the symptoms within a family that are causing the current problem. Strategic family therapy encourages the counselor to assume a more controlling role throughout the counseling process. It is designed to identify the specific current problem and create a plan to address that problem. In this way, strategic family therapy may be more effective for short-term treatment, as problems are identified and interventions are created more quickly than within other theoretical frameworks. It may also be useful in dealing with very specific issues that come up within families (e.g., school refusal) that need to be quickly addressed and solved.

The strategic family therapist will be primarily concerned with a client's current issue, placing an emphasis on specifically identifying the source of discomfort for the client and developing a plan to address that issue. Although there may be connections between the current issue and the client's past, the focus of the therapeutic work would remain on the present-day concern, not on experiences in the client's past that might pertain to that issue.

In the case of a client who has lived or is currently living with an individual who has an SUD, the counselor would help the client accurately identify the presenting issue. If the issue was directly related to living with a substance-abusing individual, the counselor might seek to assist the client in developing a plan to manage that situation in a way that promotes increased functioning and well-being. Another example might be a case where the client is exploring ways to end a relationship with an individual struggling with an SUD. In this case, the counselor would likely work with the client to develop a strategy for achieving that goal.

In a case where a client presented with an issue tied to the experience of living with a substance abuser in the past, this particular issue is not likely to become a focus of the therapy. In this case, the strategic therapist is likely to encourage the client to stay focused on the ways in which this experience is manifesting in the present. For example, if a client were experiencing issues in close relationships that he or she linked to past experiences of living with a family member with an SUD, the counselor might suggest directly addressing the issues associated with the client's present-day relationships. In this case, the client and the counselor would be likely to develop a plan to address the issues that are preventing the development of successful relationships. This plan might include behavioral steps that the client would be encouraged to take in order to change his or her current circumstances and reality.

Characteristics of Families Affected by SUD

Given these theoretical frameworks from which the counselor might conceptualize working with family members of substance abusers, several questions still remain: How does a professional counselor use these theories when working with families affected by the SUD of one of its members? And how can these theories help to organize our work with these families? In order to answer these questions, we must first understand what we can expect to discover in working with traumatized families. In other words, what patterns are likely to exist in such families?

The literature suggests that there are common characteristics among families with a substance-abusing member (see Figure 1). When families operate in an ongoing state of crisis, homeostasis

Figure 1
Characteristics of Families With a
Substance-Abusing Member

is often achieved via dysfunctional patterns. In such families, the rules, roles, and expectations that provide the state of morphostasis for the family are likely to be established in response to the SUD within the family, as opposed to the actual developmental and atypical needs of the individual family members or the real-world forces that push on the family. When this situation occurs, several predictable dysfunctional patterns are likely to emerge (Catherall, 2004). These patterns tend to be organized around three overarching themes that are at the heart of any highly dysfunctional system: denial, shame, and control.

Denial

Denial is defined as a psychological defense mechanism in which confrontation with a personal problem or with reality is avoided by denying the existence of the problem or reality (Denial, n.d.). Denial has been shown to be a characteristic of families with a substance-abusing member. In fact, the denial and misreporting of substance abuse is common in families that have a member struggling with an SUD (Stein & Rogers, 2008; Walters & Rotgers, 2012).

In order to maintain equilibrium within the family, family members will often deny that there is a substance use issue. In essence, in order to continue to function, a family needs to either address the SUD and decide on how it wishes to react to it or deny the existence of the issue in order to continue to function on a day-to-day basis. In choosing denial, the family acts as if there is no substance abuse issue, when in fact this issue is likely to be the primary organizing experience within the family. Families deny the problem in a variety of ways. They oftentimes minimize the substance use issue (e.g., "She just drinks a little too much sometimes" or "He is still adjusting to his parents' divorce"). Denial serves as a means of protecting individual family members from dealing both with the substance-abusing family member and with their genuine emotional reaction to this reality.

However, denial comes at a price. In denying the existence of the SUD within the family, the members are choosing to shut out a significant reality. Thus, the family is forced to accept the dysfunction and chaos as normal or attribute it to another family attribute or issue. Neither response is genuine, and both require a skewing of reality. Denial is especially damaging for children for a number of reasons. Predominantly egocentric, children are at great risk of attributing family dysfunction to themselves. In addition, denial requires the keeping of a large secret. If a family is invested in denying the existence of a SUD, it becomes a topic that is off limits. Therefore, a developing child has no means of processing the chaos within the family and no outlet for the feelings associated with this experience (Friel & Friel, 2010).

Shame

The secret-keeping rule associated with maintaining denial within a family that has a substance-abusing individual inevitably leads to shame. *Shame* is defined as "the painful feeling arising from the consciousness of something dishonorable, improper, ridiculous, etc., done by oneself or another" (Shame, n.d.). In the case of family members of substance abusers, the shame is not linked to specific actions or behaviors. Instead, it often exists as a shared ethos among family members (Cohen-Filipic, 2014; Rafferty & Hartley, 2006). When people (and children in particular) are told to keep a secret, the logical internal response is shame. We are not generally required to keep large secrets for long periods of time that relate to inane or inconsequential matters. We usually keep secrets when we feel deeply that there is something that we must hide in order to stay safe. Therefore, when something is happening that requires a family pact of secrecy, the family members all assume that there is something shameful about that particular attribute—and thus about them as individuals. The shame is internalized for each of the family members (Rafferty & Hartley, 2006). Deeply ingrained, shame permeates the lives of those who have a substance-abusing family member (Devine, 2013). The issue of shame is further explored when developmental theory is covered in Chapter 5. Specifically, that chapter looks at how shame develops and the impact it has on subsequent developmental growth.

Control

Control is a hallmark within families with a substance-abusing member (McIlveen, 2014). The result of both denial and shame is control. There is a tremendous amount of energy required to maintain denial, and shame produces an intolerable inner experience that individuals will attempt to control in almost any way possible. Control can take the form of rigid and immovable boundaries. In these cases, families will create routines that provide a structure that is firm and inflexible. Perhaps these families will stress the importance of following strict schedules, or they may use a set of rules that are rigidly enforced under all circumstances. At the other extreme, families may appear to have no boundaries. In these families, there may be very few expectations, and individual family members may be left to establish their own norms and behavioral patterns. In this case, there is a sense that control is not possible, even where it may be beneficial to exercise it. For example, parents may have no requirements for reasonable bedtimes, no expectations that their children will complete homework, or no curfews. Both of these scenarios prohibit the creation of healthy connections within a family. Where there are rigid and unbending boundaries, members are not likely to express themselves openly. They may also develop a sense that they can control aspects of life that are not within their control. For families where control has been entirely relinquished, members are likely to feel a sense of anxiety. In this case, individuals might internalize a belief that nothing is within their control.

When families are organized around denial, shame, and control, some predictable ways of functioning ultimately are likely to emerge. Healthy families that organize predominantly around reality and the developmental needs of its members tend to function well. Although they inevitably face stress and obstacles that need to be overcome, they are able to navigate these experiences in a manner that does not promote dysfunction or chaos but instead leaves its members with a sense that problems can be managed. However, in families with a substance-abusing member—or an otherwise traumatized family—this is not the case. In organizing themselves around the overarching tenets of denial, shame, and control, such families have some predictable dysfunctional patterns that will emerge.

Emotional Dysregulation

Poor communication skills have been associated with familial substance abuse and have become a primary emphasis in the treatment of SUD (Terrion, 2015). In families that are functioning in a fairly healthy manner, communication patterns tend to be open, and the emotional responsivity of its members tends to be modulated. In other words, members are neither forced to shut down their emotional reactions to events, nor are they encouraged to respond to events with intense levels of emotional reactivity that might infringe on others' sense of security or safety. On the other hand, in dysfunctional or traumatized families, emotional dysregulation is more likely to characterize communication among members (Buckholdt, Perra, & Jobe-Shields, 2014).

Emotional dysregulation is the inability to modulate emotional responses. In other words, individuals who struggle with emotional dysregulation often respond emotionally to situations in ways that are unpredictable and outside the range of what is typically expected. Individuals with an SUD are significantly more likely to struggle with emotional dysregulation (Powers, Stevens, Fami, & Bradley, 2015), creating a dynamic within the family in which the processing of emotional content does not occur in a predictable manner. When the emotional life of a family is not well modulated, extreme methods of dealing with emotional material are likely to become the norm. In these cases, emotionally charged interactions are sometimes prohibited. The inability to express emotion often leads to a lack of connection among family members, whereby they are unable to access or express genuine emotional responses. In addition, the shame that has been adopted within the family system reinforces the notion that the individual's feelings are unimportant or shameful.

At the other extreme, the emotional dysregulation may take the form of highly charged interactions as the norm within the family. These dysfunctional families may engage in emotional discussions that are highly reactive and uncomfortable for the members. In this case, the norm becomes ratcheting up the emotional reaction, even if it is inappropriate or hurtful. In either case, individual family members are unable to develop communication skills that incorporate individual feelings while keeping the level of emotionality within a range that is comfortable for everyone involved.

Conflict Management

One of the most important skills a child can learn is the ability to resolve conflicts. Conflict in some form is inevitable; all people will encounter situations in which they must confront and work through conflicts. In healthy families, children have generally seen adults resolve conflicts in the natural course of living. They have witnessed disagreement in which the adults are able to respectfully stand their ground and work toward a solution that is acceptable for all parties. When this is the case, the child will likely internalize these skills and naturally strive to resolve conflicts in a similar manner. In families with a substance-abusing member, however, conflict tends to be higher and is likely to remain unresolved over time (Fish, Maier, & Priest, 2015). In addition, exposure to environments characterized by high levels of conflict has been shown to result in poor social skills and higher levels of psychological distress. In families with a substance-abusing member, conflict resolution may take the form of aggressive and hurtful discourse in which the adults cross boundaries and behave in an unacceptable manner (Best et al., 2014). Disagreements may be associated with shouting, name-calling, and even physical abuse.

At the other end of the spectrum, conflict avoidance has been shown to contribute to psychological symptomatology. In families with a substance-abusing member, children who learn to avoid conflict have an increased likelihood of experiencing emotional issues (Ubinger, Handal, & Massura, 2013). This increased risk might be likely to occur in families where feelings are prohibited. Members in these families may watch other members avoid conflict at all costs and may fear and avoid conflict, even in cases where it might be to their benefit to address an issue.

Relating to Others

Families that function in a healthy manner tend to have within them relationships and subsystems that work. That is, the individual family members tend to relate to each other in a balanced manner. Boundaries are clear, and family members tend to feel comfortable with the structure of the family. These factors create an environment in which the various members and subsystems relate in predictable ways that foster security and growth (Hopsicker, 2014; Minuchin, 2006). However, in families that include a member who struggles with an SUD, low cohesion (i.e., a lack of healthy emotional bonds) and low adaptability (i.e., an incapacity to adapt their power structures, roles, relationships, and rules in response to situational and developmental concerns) are likely to characterize relationships (Van Ryzin, Fosco, & Dishion, 2012). These dysfunctional patterns lead to difficult family relationships and have been linked to adolescent substance use (Tafa & Baiocco, 2009)

In traumatized families, the relationships among individual members tend to be highly enmeshed or extremely distant (Kelley et al., 2010). When denial, shame, and control underlie the functioning of a family, it is difficult for individuals to develop open, honest, and healthy relationships with each other. At one extreme, the members of the family may be disconnected in a manner that discourages meaningful relationships. When disconnection is supported within a family, the members may learn how to relate in this manner and find it difficult to create and maintain intimate connections as they move out of the family environment. At the other extreme, the family rules may include covert expectations that the members must feel, think, and behave as one, creating an enmeshed system in which it is difficult to differentiate or establish a unique identity. In either case, the acquisition of skills required for healthy relating is thwarted, leaving the individual unable to navigate relationships in a healthy manner (LePoire, 2004).

Balancing Care of Self and Others

In families that are functioning well, children naturally develop the capacity to regulate the balance of caring for themselves and caring for others. When children's needs are met, their feelings are validated, and appropriate expectations regarding caring about the needs and feelings of others are clear, the children eventually internalize a balanced sense of taking care of themselves and meeting the needs of others. This balance is extremely important to overall psychological well-being. In fact, a lack of self-care has been linked to depression (Fullagar & O'Brien, 2014).

In families with a substance-abusing member, however, it is unlikely that the feelings of any family members will be considered on a consistent basis. In fact, inconsistency is characteristic of such families, and children are likely to experience periods of parental rejection (Pomini et al., 2014). When neglect or rejection are experienced as a part of typical family interactions, the development of a healthy sense of self is thwarted, and individuals are likely to internalize a sense of low self-esteem (Backer-Fulghum, Patock-Peckham, King, Toufa, & Hagen, 2012). Low self-esteem is incompatible with high or even healthy levels of self-care. Individuals exposed to neglect are likely to find their place in their family by always attending to the needs of others at the expense of their own well-being, or they may become very self-absorbed, feeling that they must take care of their own needs at all costs. Either extreme will set the child up for establishing future relationships that fit the pattern they have adopted.

Roles Within Families Affected by SUD

In her book *Another Chance: Hope and Health for the Alcoholic Family*, Wegscheider-Cruse (1989) proposed that because of the rigidity often associated with addiction in families, roles are covertly assigned to family members. She suggested that these roles assist the family in maintaining homeostasis. However, there is a price associated with these roles: They affect development and functioning for the individual family members. Although alternative ideas for conceptualizing the family with a substance-abusing member have been proposed, this framework continues to be used in working with clients from families with a substance-abusing member (Middleton-Moz & Dwinell, 2010; see Table 3).

Table 3
Roles in Families With a Substance-Abusing Member

Label and Description	Role Within Family	Consequence
Addict		
The person with the SUD	The focal point around which the family is organized	Continued substance abuse/addiction
Enabler		
The individual (typically the partner, although it can be a child) who covers for the addict in ways that allow the addictive behavior to continue	Maintains the equilibrium within the family by ensuring that no change will occur	Shame, guilt, exhaustion, inability to live an authentic existence
Hero		
The individual (very often an older child) who makes the family look good. Usually a high achiever who follows the rules	To preserve the image of the family to the public	Perfectionism, shame; identity that is linked to achievements
Lost child		
The individual (often a middle child) who "fades into the woodwork"; attempts to disappear and need nothing	To alleviate the pressures within the family by not needing attention or care	Loneliness, disconnection, a sense of worthlessness.
Scapegoat		
The individual (often a middle child) who attempts to divert the attention of the family by acting out	To behave in a manner that draws the attention of the family to themselves	Poor school performance, behavioral issues, substance abuse
Mascot		
The individual (often a youngest child) who uses humor to redirect the family's emotional responses; often uses silly behavior or humor	To help the family keep things lighter, thus diverting attention from the addiction	Shame, disconnection; identity linked to humor, sometimes masking genuine feelings

Note. Based on the work of Wegscheider-Cruse (1989). SUD = substance use disorder.

The Addict

The addict is said to possess the central role within the family system; this is the person struggling with an SUD. As previously mentioned, a family with an addicted member tends to organize itself around the addiction. The dynamics that are ultimately created within the family serve to support the substance abuse behavior, and the addict becomes central within the system. Thus, the individual with the SUD tends to behave erratically and is often irresponsible. Therefore, that person cannot be depended upon to provide consistent support of any kind, and this situation is thought to encourage the rigid formation of other roles.

The Enabler

The enabler is said to provide the means for maintaining the addiction within the family and thus supports the formation and maintenance of the other roles. Often referred to as *codependent* (a construct that is fully described in Chapter 6), the enabler is likely to take on a caretaking role within the family, working to make sure that family members' needs are met despite the presence of the addiction within the family. Oftentimes, the enabler is the adult partner of the addict. However, a parent of an addict can be an enabler as can a child with a substance-abusing parent. The enabler's primary role is to support a façade of normalcy. This individual is likely to make excuses for the person with the SUD. For example, the enabler might tell an employer or a school that the member with the SUD is physically ill when, in fact, the substance abuser is unable to meet his or her responsibilities because he or she is abusing substances. In addition, the enabler will work to maintain the family's image, expending a great deal of energy ensuring that the family secret is maintained.

For the enabler, the underlying feelings tend to be inadequacy, fear, and helplessness. Because the SUD is the reality within the family, the enabler is inevitably going to fail. With substance abuse at the center of family functioning, the enabler will not be able to successfully carry out his or her role. In particular, meeting the needs of the other family members is not possible when the primary need (i.e., the need for the family to be free of the organizing substance abuse issue) can never be met. Therefore, the enabler is set up to feel inadequate. In addition, the enabler lives in fear—primarily fear of the family's secret being discovered. Finally, the enabler lives with a feeling of helplessness. Despite the enabler's best efforts, the family continues to be wounded and damaged.

The Hero

The hero's primary responsibility within a family with a substance-abusing member is to make the family look good. Likely to become a perfectionist, the hero believes that if he or she can attain perfection, it can affect the dysfunction within the family. Often an older child in the family, the hero quickly learns that it is his or her job to excel, even at the expense of his or her own well-being. The hero is likely to be a leader; to be successful in academics, sports, or some other socially acceptable pursuit; and to be serious and driven.

The price for the hero is that he or she is likely to feel excessive fear, guilt, and shame. As with the enabler, a part of the hero's role is to protect the family secret and assist the family in appearing normal, or even extraordinary. This responsibility is likely to be associated with fear that the secret will emerge or with an intense fear of failure. With the hero's identity inextricably tied to his or her ability to be successful, failure would result in a feeling of having let the family down by not living up to the role expectations. In addition, the hero's sense of self could be crushed by even a perceived failure.

Heroes are also likely to attempt to rescue the family. If they are perfect enough, perhaps the family can be healed. This overdeveloped sense of power and responsibility leads to feelings of guilt and shame. When they are not successful at healing the family, they are likely to internalize this experience as shame and feel that they must be defective in some manner. This feeling can create a cycle whereby the hero attempts perfection to make the family better, fails at fixing the family, feels enormous shame and fear, and tries again to achieve the perfection he or she is sure is required to heal the family.

The Lost Child

The lost child in a family with a substance-abusing member is the child who is rarely noticed. His or her job within the family is to need very little and stay out of the way. The lost child is likely to play alone and appear aloof. This child may not have many friends and will likely appear "fine." It has been said that this is the child who sits in the back of the classroom and whose name teachers will still not know, long after they are able to identify all of the other children in their class. The lost child will master the art of fading into the woodwork and can therefore be easily forgotten.

The underlying feelings of the lost child can include anger, loneliness, and neglect. Although the lost children are likely to perpetuate the belief that they do not have any imminent needs, as children, this is of course not the case. All children possess a multitude of needs, including the need to be recognized and seen. Therefore, a feeling of rage is likely to accompany the satisfied demeanor that the lost child presents to the world. They are also likely to feel lonely, as they are rarely noticed. Finally, because they are so often neglected, they may feel that they are not worthy.

The Scapegoat

The scapegoat in a family with a substance-abusing member pulls the family's attention toward them. Often this is the child who acts out and misbehaves. This behavior serves to divert the family from the SUD, as the chaos often created by the scapegoat consumes the attention of the adults in the family. The scapegoat is likely to be a risk taker and get into trouble. The scapegoat can also be a leader. However, he or she is likely to be admired by individuals who are also interested in acting out as a means of attaining power or status.

The scapegoat is likely to feel shame, guilt, and emptiness. Oftentimes, the scapegoat begins to act out in response to feelings of emptiness and shame. These children are likely to feel that they are not good enough and that nothing they do will ever be good enough. In response to this internal struggle, scapegoats may choose to attain their sense of worthiness using negative behaviors, thus averting the shameful feelings. In acting out and being labeled the family misfit or failure, they can create an identity. However, at the same time, scapegoats are likely to know that their behavior is unacceptable, increasing the emptiness that fuels their shame.

The Mascot

The mascot's purpose within the family is to use humor to divert attention away from the SUD. The mascot provides the comic relief necessary for enduring the stress that is ever-present within a family affected by SUD. However, the humor provided is not always perceived as funny by all of the family members, as oftentimes the mascot's humor can be at another's expense. However, the mascot is likely to be popular and well liked (both inside and outside of the family), possessing a personality that draws others to him or her. Mascots will often assume the role of class clown and will be perceived as funny and light-hearted.

However, underneath the humor, the mascot is likely to harbor embarrassment, shame, and anger. Mascots will often struggle with the belief that if they were ever to lose this particular source of identity (i.e., their ability to make others laugh), they would be abandoned. This fear inevitably leads to anger, as they never feel validated for who they are, only for their ability to lighten the mood. It will also lead the mascot to feel embarrassment and shame, as they believe that their worthiness is dependent upon their ability to provide comic relief and that they are never truly seen.

Although these roles provide a framework for understanding specific behaviors and feelings for a client, this model is not without its critics (Vernig, 2011). Critics of this model primarily suggest that it does not capture the depth of experience for individuals in families with a substance-abusing member. In addition, it presents the possible roles in a manner that might be construed as fixed, when in fact family members do not necessarily ascribe to one role in a rigid manner that excludes the possibility of moving into different roles as circumstances and individuals within the system change and develop.

There is also virtually no evidence supporting the existence of these roles, as attempts to measure these constructs have fallen short. Finally, there is no evidence supporting the existence of these roles in diverse or even blended families.

A more recent model that seems to be gaining traction is the narrative model (Payne, 2006). In exploring the experiences of clients from families with a substance-abusing member, a counselor using narrative therapy separates the individual from specific attributes or defining characteristics. Through the telling of stories and the application of meaning making to those accounts, the therapist and client gain a rich and complex picture of how the client has navigated the world—a method that tends to minimize the impact of specific labels. According to Singer, Singer, and Berry (2013), the use of this model in working with individuals with an SUD has allowed both clients and counselors to engage in a process where they can begin to conceptualize the addiction within the life of the client in a way that maximizes an understanding of the complex nature of how it is woven into all of the other facets of the client's life. In doing so, the client is theoretically able to avoid seeing himself or herself as a "role" and can instead begin to understand how he or she navigated the vast array of circumstances within his or her life in a number of ways, perhaps including the adoption of particular roles when this was beneficial.

Case Example for Family Theory

Marshall has come for counseling at the university counseling center. He is a 21-year-old mixed-race college senior who is experiencing extreme anxiety related to his upcoming graduation. Marshall will receive his bachelor's degree in communications with a minor in business management. He is currently looking for postgraduation employment and is not experiencing success. He has been working with a counselor in the Career Planning and Placement Office on the campus, who suggested that he might want to speak with a counselor at the Counseling Center regarding his anxiety.

Marshall is a commuter student at the university, where over 95% of the undergraduate population lives on campus. He reports having felt somewhat disconnected from the university experience throughout his years as a college student. In addition, the majority of students who attend the university are Caucasian (87%), further adding to his sense of alienation. Marshall describes feeling anxious throughout this entire educational experience, always feeling that he had to prove himself and fearing that he would be excluded. As a result, Marshall admits that he did not make much of an effort throughout his undergraduate experience to reach out to fellow students or to faculty members. He regrets this now, as he wonders if the job search process would be easier if he had pushed himself to move outside of his comfort zone. At this point, Marshall reports that his sole focus is on finding a job, stating that his parents will be very upset if he is unable to gain employment. As he begins to talk about his parents, Marshall seems to become increasingly anxious.

Reflection

Initially, the counselor may begin to perceive Marshall's anxiety as somewhat typical, as anxiety around the job search process is expected among college seniors. However, within the context of feeling disconnected from the university community and worrying about the likelihood of being accepted, the anxiety might be perceived as more complex. The counselor is likely to want to explore these issues with Marshall in an effort to better understand his current anxiety as well as to illuminate for him some connections that might be taking place. In addition, the counselor is likely to pick up on Marshall's increased level of anxiety associated with talking about his parents. This represents another avenue that the counselor may wish to explore.

As Marshall continues to tell his story, he begins to talk more about his family. Marshall grew up in a city that shares a boundary with the upper-middle-class suburban town in which the university is located. He is the fourth of five children in a blended family. He currently lives with his biological mother, Angela, a 42-year-old Haitian American who moved to the United States at the age of 12; his stepfather, Nelson; his maternal grandmother; and his 16-year-old half sister, Anastasia. At the age of 19, Angela (Marshall's mother) married Andre, an African American who grew up in the neighborhood where Marshall lives now, and they had three children. Shortly after the birth of their third child, Angela and Andre were divorced. A year later, Angela married Chris, a Caucasian man; they had two children, the older of whom is Marshall. When Marshall was 9 years old, Chris and Angela divorced, presumably because Chris was addicted to cocaine. Three years after her divorce from Chris (Marshall's biological father), when Marshall was 12, Angela married his current stepfather, Nelson. Since that time, Marshall has had no contact with his biological father; he has lived with his mother, Nelson, his maternal grandmother, and his 16-year-old half sister, Anastasia.

Marshall describes his home life as tense. He claims that his stepfather is a raging alcoholic, and that the rest of the family lives in fear of his drinking. He claims that Nelson has been unable to keep a steady job because of his drinking, which has created an inconsistent and often stressful financial situation for the family. Marshall's mother works in a school cafeteria during the day and is able to pick up a few shifts a week at a neighborhood bar. Marshall has attempted to talk his mother into leaving Nelson but to no avail. His mother accuses

Marshall of exaggerating, saying that Nelson is simply under stress and drinks every so often when this is the case. She has also told Marshall not to discuss family affairs with anyone outside of the family.

Marshall begins to cry and tells the counselor that this is in fact the very first time he has ever told anyone about his family life. He reports feeling intense shame at divulging this family secret and begins to explain that he feels like a failure. When the counselor probes to further understand this feeling, Marshall shares that he has always known that it was his job to succeed and thus make the family look good. He is reminded of the sacrifices his mother has made to ensure that he received his college degree, and he recalls the many instances in which she bragged about him to other family members. At his point, Marshall is terrified of not fulfilling his obligation to his family, and he feels that this is a distinct possibility, as he has thus far been unable to find employment.

Implications for the Counselor

Marshall describes a stressful childhood filled with numerous transitions. The counselor is likely to begin the counseling process with Marshall with a primary focus on both establishing a therapeutic relationship with Marshall and developing a clear understanding of Marshall's story. Specifically, the counselor will want to use accurate empathy to ascertain Marshall's emotional reactions to the family stresses he describes. This process will likely take some time, and the counselor may want to use a genogram to visually depict the various relationships within Marshall's family.

In addition, the counselor will likely want to explore the shame response that Marshall has expressed. An understanding of the origins of this shame and how it was internalized for Marshall will help the counselor to better understand Marshall's present-day struggles. Once the counselor has a clear and accurate sense of Marshall's story from his perspective, a more structured approach to the counseling process may be indicated. The counselor can use a variety of theoretical frameworks in initiating this phase of the counseling process.

Discussion Questions

1. What assumptions might you make about Marshall's family with regard to equilibrium? How has equilibrium been maintained in the various iterations of Marshall's family life?
2. Apply the family theories discussed to Marshall's case, and describe how they might be incorporated into counseling.
3. How do you see denial, shame, and control manifested within Marshall's family and for Marshall specifically?
4. In which areas is this family having the most difficulty functioning?

Chapter 5

Developmental Theory

As professional counselors, we are committed to assessing and treating clients through the lens of developmental theory. Consideration of both typical and atypical development is critical to the counseling process. We use a variety of theoretical perspectives to conceptualize development and to identify the typical struggles and tasks for periods across the life span. In using these models, professional counselors are also able to identify atypical experiences, which are often the result of environmental circumstances that impact the developmental process.

This chapter explores the application of developmental theory to working with families that have a substance-abusing member. In addressing this particular topic, it is important to consider the distinction between children whose parents or siblings have an SUD and adults who live with a substance-abusing family member. The experience of living with a family member struggling with an SUD is more intense for a developing child than for an adult. In the event that a child lives in a system organized around the substance abuse issue of a particular member, the developmental implications make this experience far more influential than the same experience would be for an adult who spent the early developmental periods in an environment free of this experience, especially when the earlier developmental periods were spent in a relatively healthy environment in which needs were consistently met. Children are far more vulnerable to the environment than adults. Humans construct their view of the world, their place in that world, and the neurobiological mechanisms for supporting this activity primarily within the early developmental life stages. Although these things can change across the life span, it is during this time that children internalize their experiences and begin to respond emotionally, socially, and biologically to these internalized messages and meanings. These experiences then form the basis upon which future environmental stimuli will be processed and understood (Broderick & Blewitt, 2014). Therefore, in the case of children whose parent, or even a sibling, is struggling with an SUD, the potential for long-term consequences and issues is heightened.

In fact, the most well-researched population of individuals who live with a substance-abusing family member are children of substance abusers. In particular, substantial attention has been given to the population of children of alcoholics (COAs). Of course, COAs constitute a diverse population of individuals with varying circumstances that affect their response to parental substance abuse. However, despite the unique circumstances for individuals raised by a parent with an SUD, the consensus in the field of substance abuse and addictions is that this population of individuals struggles with a number of identified issues at a significantly higher rate than individuals who are not raised by substance-abusing parents. In fact, this conclusion has been empirically tested over a number of years, and the literature supports this assumption (Klostermann et al., 2011; Menees & Segrin, 2000; Sher, Walitzer, Wood, & Brent, 1991). These issues span all facets of an individual's life and include psychiatric diagnoses that occur at higher rates for COAs as well as feelings, thoughts, and behaviors that affect development throughout the life span. It is therefore critical to synthesize our foundational understanding of how human development is affected when the family environment is organized around an SUD.

Many theories of development have been proposed and studied, and all of them provide important perspectives. However, it is not feasible to present all of these perspectives in this book. Therefore, in this book I limit the exploration and application of developmental perspectives to psychosocial development, as this is perhaps the area of development that counselors are most likely to explore with clients. In this chapter I provide a brief overview of Eric Erikson's theory of psychosocial development (1950), as it is a widely accepted psychosocial model for conceptualizing client cases. In addition, Erikson's theory links seamlessly to the kinds of issues that might present in working with clients dealing with the issue of familial substance abuse.

Erik Erikson is credited with the development of a psychosocial theory built on the work of Sigmund Freud (1930/2010). Erikson asserted that Freud emphasized particular aspects of development while avoiding others (Erikson, 1950), and Erikson developed a theory that he felt provided a more balanced view of the psychosocial development of individuals. In addition, Erikson expanded the notion of development, continuing it into later stages and proposing a life span perspective. As professional counselors, we endorse a life span perspective; thus, Erikson's theory has played a large role in our professional understanding of human development.

Erikson proposed eight stages of development. He characterized each of these stages with a specific crisis. However, he did not see the developmental crisis as a catastrophe or negative experience. Instead, he proposed a continuum of two opposing outcomes for each developmental stage. The identified crisis represents what Erikson saw as the central theme or life task typical of individuals within that developmental stage. Furthermore, he suggested that optimal development within a particular stage would result in a resolution of the identified crisis that was positive (i.e., at one end of the continuum). Poor resolution of the crisis would result in a negative outcome (i.e., the other end of the continuum). In reality, individuals will resolve each developmental crisis with a greater or lesser degree of success in terms of overall psychosocial development. As counselors, we can benefit greatly by assessing the developmental histories of our clients. To be specific, we can put present-day issues into context when we understand what may have transpired for a client during critical developmental periods.

In looking at Erikson's eight stages of development, we are primarily concerned with what we might anticipate in the case of a client who was affected by familial substance abuse during particular developmental stages.

Children develop, at least partly, in response to their environment. In fact, they are dependent upon their environment to support their development. When that environment includes stressors that either require the single-minded attention of the adult caregivers, or result in deleterious experiences (e.g., ongoing conflict, violence, etc.), the developmental needs of the child may be neglected. For example, in cases where marital discord, financial stress, housing instability, or mental illness is part of a family's life, children's development is adversely affected (Nievar, Moske, Johnson, & Chen, 2014). An SUD represents a significant mental health issue and will inevitably affect the development of children within the family. In addition, the other stressors mentioned (marital discord, financial stress, and housing instability) are often co-occurring with the substance abuse in a family, compounding the developmental impact on children raised in this particular environment (Chan, Doan, & Tompson, 2014; Moore, Biegel, & McMahon, 2011).

In light of the multitude of struggles likely to be characteristic of families with a substance-abusing member, children in these families are at particular risk. In fact, researchers have shown that psychiatric diagnoses occur at higher rates for children of parents with an SUD; in addition, there are differences in brain circuitry related to impulse control between children of substance-abusing parents and those of non-substance-abusing parents (Hardee et al., 2014; Park & Schepp, 2014). Thus, parental SUD is likely to affect relationships throughout the lives of children raised in such an environment, and it can contribute to a lower level of psychological well-being across the life span.

The specific issues linked to living with an individual with an SUD are covered in subsequent chapters. However, as one considers the implications of this life circumstance using a developmental framework, it is important to stress some of the differences that are linked specifically to developmental experiences. As mentioned, the impact of being raised from birth by a primary caregiver struggling with an SUD will differ from the impact of choosing a substance-abusing adult partner after a childhood spent in a family that did not include substance abuse (Hussong, Zucker, Wong, Fitzgerald, & Puttler, 2005; Schuckit, Smith, Pierson, Trim, & Danko, 2008). The developmental process for a child raised by a substance-abusing parent can be affected in such a way that the child is unable to achieve mastery in a manner that fosters the development of a healthy and autonomous identity (Liota, 2012). It is therefore important for the counselor to be mindful of the presence of substance abuse in the client's life in the context of developmental expectations. For example, for the client who reports a stable and uneventful childhood but recalls all of that changing when his or her father started drinking during the client's teenage years, the counselor might assume that the earlier developmental tasks were mastered within an environment that was free of SUD as well as the resulting chaos associated with this experience. However, if the same client reported that his or her mother drank throughout the client's entire childhood, the conceptualization of the case would change dramatically. In this case, the counselor would assume that all of this client's developmental mastery—until the time he or she may have left home—took place in an environment where SUD played a central role. That is, the client's primary caregiver was struggling with an SUD throughout all of the client's childhood developmental stages. As we explore the developmental stages, these differences are highlighted in order to illuminate the potential impact of familial substance abuse.

Erik Erikson's Theory of Psychosocial Development

Trust vs. Mistrust

Erikson's first stage of psychosocial development takes place throughout the first year of life. The crisis, or developmental task, is that of trust vs. mistrust. Within this developmental stage, children will be mastering the psychosocial task of trust, or developing a basis for seeing the world as a safe place where their needs will be met. The positive resolution of this developmental crisis will result in a foundation whereby children assume that essentially they will be cared for in ways that assure their safety and comfort.

In the case where an individual is being raised in a family with a substance-abusing member, the development of trust can be very precarious. For example, consider a situation in which the mother is struggling with an SUD and is acting as the primary caregiver to a child. It is unlikely that the infant will receive consistent care. Previously, I touched upon the importance of a secure attachment to the achievement of optimal psychological well-being. In fact, according to Bowlby (2004), the establishment of a healthy attachment between a primary caregiver and the infant is essential to the development of both trust and a healthy sense of self. In addition, this very early attachment experience is said to lay the groundwork for future relationships. In a case where the primary caregiver has an SUD, attachment is challenging, as it requires an emotionally available and constant presence for the infant (Mate, 2010). It is unlikely that a primary caregiver struggling with an SUD will be able to provide this kind of care. In the case where the substance-abusing family member is not the primary caregiver, inconsistency in care and high levels of anxiety are still likely to exist. Although the impact on the successful resolution of this psychosocial developmental stage may not be affected to the same degree that it is when the primary caregiver is the substance-abusing family member, it is unlikely that an environment that consistently supports the development of trust will be created or maintained. In either case, a positive resolution to this initial developmental crisis may be thwarted and trust issues may be at the core of such a client's presenting issues. In fact, issues with trust among COAs have been shown to extend into young adulthood, suggesting that the quality of resolution of this developmental crisis may affect children from families with a substance-abusing member well into their futures (Larson, Holt, Wilson, Medora, & Newell, 2001).

Autonomy vs. Shame and Doubt

During the second and third year of life, children face the crisis associated with autonomy vs. shame and doubt. With the development of an initial and primitive ability to see oneself as separate from the primary caregiver, the young child will strive for a sense of autonomy. Thus, the key to the successful resolution of this developmental crisis is supporting the child's sense of autonomy while providing limits that keep the child safe and secure.

When a family member has an SUD, dysfunction is likely to exist. During this very important developmental stage, the child is experiencing his or her initial sense of autonomy—understanding for the first time that he or she is separate from the primary caregiver. This discovery is likely to include a sense of curiosity and a desire to begin exploring the world. Without any internal mechanism for controlling behavior, the 1- or 2-year-old is dependent upon care-givers to establish safe and reasonable boundaries while encouraging positive attempts at autonomous functioning. When substance abuse is a primary issue within a family, caregivers are likely to be preoccupied and distracted. If this is the case, the child might be neglected, with few or no limits placed on behavior. Hence, the child is likely to experience terror as he or she attempts to explore the environment without having the safety provided by reasonable limits. At the other extreme, children in dysfunctional families are sometimes harshly disciplined as a means of controlling the chaos within the family. In this case, the behavioral expectations may be unreasonable and inappropriate for a 2- or 3-year-old child. When toddlers are harshly punished or no limits are placed on their be-havior, the psychological response is shame (Dunn et al., 2002).

As we have discussed, shame is characteristic of families organized around one family member's SUD. Thus, the inter-nalization of shame is likely for children in such families and is initiated in this developmental stage. Both neglect and expec-tations that are unattainable cause shame for the developing child. From a clinical perspective this shame might be revealed as an ongoing and pervasive sense of low self-worth. As profes-sional counselors, you may see clients later in life who present with self-images that reflect shame. They may manifest as an overdeveloped sense of responsibility, whereby the client feels guilty and responsible for events and circumstances that are not within his or her control. Or a client may simply report feeling worthless and consistently afraid that others will discover his or her inadequacies. In working with clients who possess high levels of shame, counselors will want to gain an understanding of the origins of the shame. This understanding will promote a clearer interpretation of clients' present-day application of their shame-based approach to life. In the event that the shame is the result of family dynamics that the client could not control or influence (e.g., a substance use issue within the family), a cognitive approach might help the client consider the rationality of his or her present-day issues with shame.

Initiative vs. Guilt

This third stage of development, initiative vs. guilt, takes place throughout the preschool years (ages 3–6). During this stage, the child who has experienced positive resolution of the previous devel-opmental crises will begin to show and develop initiative. Initiative is characterized by a natural sense of curiosity. If prior developmental stages were met with frustration or resolved negatively, the child at this stage is likely to experience high levels of guilt that might keep them from freely exploring their environment.

Because these developmental stages are sequential and build upon the quality of the resolution of previous stages, what has already transpired within the life of a child is likely to affect the resolution of subsequent developmental crises. For example, in the event that a child is being raised in a family where SUD is playing a central role, he or she is likely to enter this developmental stage with some level of both mistrust and shame.

As mentioned above, during this stage of development, we expect children to display a sense of initiative, which is likely to manifest itself with an increased level of curiosity and desire to explore and understand the world. The child is likely to be highly inquisitive and ask questions on an ongoing basis, requiring patience and focused attention on the part of caregivers. The successful resolution of this stage is dependent upon experiences that result in a feeling of accomplishment or mastery. In a family where one of the members has an SUD, it is unlikely that this kind of joyous exploration will be encouraged or rewarded. In fact, in families that are struggling intensely, there may be discouragement, or even punishment, for behaviors that are typical and expected within this stage of development. In this case, the child is likely to develop an increased sense of internalized shame in the form of guilt.

Industry vs. Inferiority

Throughout the early school years (ages 6–11), children will move into the industry vs. inferiority stage of development. The developmental task in this stage is to become industrious. Children who have had positive experiences prior to this stage of development will engage in learning and begin to see themselves as contributors who are able to succeed in a learning environment. When the previous developmental milestones have not been resolved successfully, the internalized mistrust, shame, or guilt is likely to encourage a sense of inferiority.

For a child with a substance-abusing family member, this developmental stage is likely to be challenging. It is during this stage of development that children begin school. As a child begins this important activity, which will remain an integral of his or her development for many years, a sense of industry is important to a successful outcome. From a theoretical standpoint, when prior developmental stages have been successfully resolved, this sense of industry and desire to work at learning and being successful in school evolves naturally (with the possible exception of children who struggle with specific learning issues). However, in a case where the child has gone through the prior developmental stages while living with a family member who has an SUD, it is likely that the child will enter this stage feeling ambivalent about the world and having internalized a sense of not being good enough. In this case, the child is at risk of feeling inferior, even if he or she is academically successful.

Identity vs. Identity Confusion

The next developmental stage, according to Erikson, involves the resolution of the crisis related directly to identity development: identity vs. identity confusion. This stage encompasses adolescence (ages 12–18). It is during this time that children strive to establish an identity in the world. Through experimentation with roles and the development of more awareness of the world, the adolescent will naturally attempt to discover where he or she fits and will establish an initial identity.

For the adolescent who has been raised in a family where SUD has been the primary organizing factor, the process of identity development can be very difficult. For one thing, this child is likely to have entered this stage of development without having resolved previous developmental crises in a way that supports healthy identity development. In addition, as discussed earlier, families with a substance-abusing member frequently do not support individuation or differentiation. Furthermore, in a system where there are secrets to maintain, autonomous identity development among individual members may threaten the equilibrium of the family system. Identity development is dependent upon how people see themselves within their family and how they view themselves in relationships with others. In the case where an adolescent has adopted and rigidly held a role within his or her family (i.e., enabler, hero, lost child, scapegoat, mascot), that adolescent's identity and sense of self will likely reflect this role. Likewise, if the adolescent is part of a system where differentiation of self is not supported, the establishment of a healthy separate identity is likely to be difficult.

Intimacy vs. Isolation

During young adulthood, individuals are likely to struggle with intimacy vs. isolation. It is during this time that the developing individual will strive to establish intimacy in important relationships. Erikson suggested that real intimacy is not possible without the formation of an identity. Therefore, it is during this time that individuals, having theoretically developed an identity during adolescence, can succeed in the development of genuine intimate relationships.

As individuals raised in families with a substance-abusing member enter adulthood, it is likely that at least some of the previous developmental struggles have not been resolved effectively, leaving them at high risk for intimacy issues. Theoretically, it is during this stage that individuals will begin to establish their adult lives in the world. A substantial part of this process involves developing a variety of relationships that will serve as a social support network and may include relationships that will define a new family. As discussed previously, Bowen (1978) would suggest that individuals within this stage of development are likely to be attracted to and to attract significant others at a level of differentiation similar to their own. How an individual chooses others for intimate relationships is highly dependent upon how they see themselves in the world. How they view themselves in the world and in relationship to and with others is likely a product of many factors, including how they navigated previous developmental crises within their families. The resolution of prior developmental stages is intricately connected to one's ability for intimate connection with others. This interplay between resolution of prior developmental struggles and current-day psychological well-being is complicated and needs to be explored and understood for each client.

Generativity vs. Stagnation

During middle age (40s–early 60s), the developing individual is likely to struggle with generativity vs. stagnation. During this stage of development, most adults will feel a pull toward contributing to the world in some way. For many adults, this impulse takes the form of raising their own children. However, this pull can also manifest itself through engagement in community work or employment that feels meaningful. For individuals who are not able to resolve this development stage in a positive manner, there is likely to be a sense of stagnation. Those individuals may feel that they have been unable to accomplish what they had hoped to accomplish, and they may experience a sense of being stuck and unable to achieve a sense of generativity.

It is difficult to predict the developmental struggles for individuals in this stage of development who were raised in families with a substance-abusing member, as there are a multitude of factors that will affect the resolution of this particular crisis. For example, has the individual worked to resolve issues prior to this stage? Has the individual participated in individual or group counseling that may have helped him or her resolve prior tasks effectively? In addition, there are numerous life events that can support or interfere with a sense of generativity. For example, divorce, aging parents, and economic struggles or successes all have an impact on how adults navigate this stage in their lives.

From a counseling perspective, it may not be beneficial to unilaterally categorize individuals raised in families with a substance-abusing member. Instead, it may be helpful to hear a client's story in order to determine how that individual may have come to experience whatever struggle has brought him or her into counseling. By listening to the client's story and considering the developmental struggles and successes that client has experienced throughout life, the counselor—working with the client—may be able to link previous developmental experiences with current-day struggles.

Integrity vs. Despair

The final stage of development described by Erikson is that of integrity vs. despair. In this final stage of life (older adulthood), the task of the developing individual revolves around the integration of life experiences. In the case where an older adult is able to experience a sense of integrity, it is likely that this individual has been able to review his or her life and feel a sense of contentment and acceptance. These adults are likely to recognize the successes in their life and be able to integrate the hardships and "failures" in a way that leaves them feeling a sense of overall integrity. In the case where an individual feels despair, the life review is likely to be fraught with disappointment and regret, resulting in a sense that one's life has not been lived as well as one might desire.

For older adults who have experienced SUD in the family, a multitude of factors may influence how they fare in this developmental stage. If a client at this developmental stage is having difficulty integrating such an experience, such integration might become a focus of counseling. The counselor and client can work toward achieving a sense of integrity associated with this life event.

Case Example for Development Theory

Aaban is a 48-year-old Iranian male who has come for counseling for the first time in his life. He reports that he is currently in a relationship that he is very hopeful about but fears that he is likely to "screw things up." Aaban expresses this concern because of a rocky relationship history. He has been in the United States for 30 years and feels that he has grown accustomed to life here. He reports feeling generally happy, but he feels tremendous anxiety regarding relationships.

As counseling continues, Aaban begins to describe traumatic childhood experiences. He spent his childhood in Iran. He was the youngest of three children; he has an older brother and an older sister, who are 10 and 11 years older than he is, respectively. Aaban always felt as if he did not belong and wondered if his parents did not want to have him. Aaban describes his early life as "scary," and his siblings were so much older than he was that he felt isolated and alone.

Reflection

At this point, the counselor might begin to connect Aaban's childhood to his current-day struggles. His description of his childhood as both scary and lonely might suggest that early developmental tasks were difficult to master. The counselor will likely want to more fully comprehend Aaban's fears and loneliness.

As counseling continues, Aaban begins to share more of the details of his childhood experiences. He reports that his mother stayed at home, raising the children and maintaining the family home. His memories of his mother are of a timid, depressed woman who was very tired and overwhelmed much of the time. His father worked sporadically, primarily in the field of construction. Aaban describes his father as unpredictable and abusive. Aaban is not sure if his father was an alcoholic, as this was not a term he knew or understood. However, he recalls that his father "drank a lot," stayed out a lot, and often stayed in bed well into the day. When his father was awake and with the family, Aaban says that the atmosphere was tense; everyone was walking on eggshells. His father could be explosive, and predicting these episodes was impossible.

Aaban's earliest memories include his mother frantically working to make sure that everything at home was "perfect." Aaban recalls that when she "failed" in this task, his father hit and verbally assaulted her. In addition, Aaban reports several instance of being punished and "spanked" for such things as spilling a drink or failing to pick up a toy he had been playing with. He recalls school as a safe haven. However, he was extremely timid and always afraid that he would make a mistake that would be reported to his father.

Aaban decided to move to the United States when he was a young adult. He reports that although the transition was difficult, he is very happy that he made this move. Aaban initially located an Iranian community and found work through his connections there. He reports that during that time, he was continually being set up with a variety of young women, and he felt completely overwhelmed with the prospect of developing an intimate relationship. Aaban reports that he drove women away because of his fears and his inability to commit.

Eventually, Aaban was able to secure employment as the manager of a warehouse, and he claims to like his work. Recently he met a woman whom he refers to as a possible soul mate. He claims to love her very much and is terrified that he will push her away. He does not want to do this, and this is the primary motivation for seeking counseling.

Implications for the Counselor

In the case of Aaban, the counselor is likely to be struck by some of the childhood experiences Aaban described. In particular, the counselor is likely to make note of the dysfunction that seems to have been characteristic of Aaban's family. The counselor is also likely to assume that Aaban navigated every developmental crisis in a dysfunctional environment. With this in mind, the counselor will likely want to assist Aaban in conceptualizing his current-day struggles in the context of what he has learned about the world. A cognitive approach might be beneficial as a means of assessing the rationality of Aaban's perception of his current-day reality. If Aaban had difficulty resolving developmental conflicts in a positive manner, he is likely to be making assumptions about his current-day life that might not reflect reality.

Discussion Questions

1. Given Aaban's history, how might you begin to characterize his early developmental experiences?
2. In analyzing this case from a developmental perspective, in which stages might you expect Aaban has struggled?
3. How might this analysis influence your conceptualization of this case?
4. How might you make sense of Aaban's struggles with present relationships given his development history?

Chapter 6

Codependency

Earlier chapters have used several theoretical lenses to focus on the impact of substance abuse in the family. The current chapter covers literature specific to clients affected by a family member's SUD and describes the construct of codependency, which has been used to characterize this group of individuals. Specifically, in this chapter I consider the scholarly work and empirical investigation of codependency.

Introduction to Codependency

In the 1980s, a construct was identified to characterize and treat individuals involved in a close relationship with someone struggling with an SUD. The dysfunctional process linked to these individuals became known as *codependency*. At first, self-help books on this topic flooded bookstores, and eventually research and scholarly inquiry of codependency began to emerge.

The literature on codependency initially focused on investigating the impact of substance abuse on COAs. In studying this population, researchers found that COAs were at greater risk of struggling with emotional, behavioral, and relational issues than their peers who did not have alcoholic parents (Hussong et al., 2005; Schuckit et al., 2008). This line of inquiry and the movement to identify the unique characteristics and needs of COAs prompted the identification of a disease process attributable to individuals in close relationships with alcoholics and substance abusers, and the codependency movement began. Codependency became the catchword for conceptualizing a set of behaviors and issues associated with living with a substance abuser.

As a result, some researchers set out to empirically substantiate and describe the existence and features of codependency.

The scientific efforts to describe and explain codependency as a legitimate illness with a substantiated set of criteria fell short for several reasons. First, codependence by its nature is very difficult to study. A multitude of confounding variables exist, making it extremely difficult to isolate the precise impact of living with a substance abuser. For example, issues such as poverty, abuse, and relationship to the individual with the SUD represent just a few of the factors that inevitably affect the level and nature of codependency, which creates immense challenges in studying the construct. In addition, measuring the issues associated with codependency is difficult. The potential consequences of living with an individual with an SUD may include hypervigilance, depression, personality disorders, and acting out, and the method for precisely measuring these constructs is not well defined. Therefore, obtaining data that are relevant, valid, and accurate has made the empirical investigation of codependency challenging; in fact, some scholars are not convinced that the construct has been subjected to rigorous scientific inquiry (Sandoz, 2004).

In addition to the difficulties inherent in measuring codependency, the introduction of this construct prompted controversy. Both clients and helping professionals have resisted the acceptance of a label for individuals deemed ill by virtue of the illness of another. For COAs in particular, the codependency label and associated issues attributable to them have been met with resistance. The fact that COAs have been identified as ill (i.e., codependent) on the basis of having been raised by a substance-abusing parent has not been unequivocally accepted. In fact, some COAs reject the codependency label and maintain that they are not ill and in fact may possess coping strategies and a level of resiliency superior to their non-COA peers. Codependents are often extremely high-functioning individuals who have highly developed survival skills. Indeed, one of the common characteristics of codependents is that they do not easily accept help and often push forward in isolation, having therefore achieved whatever status, happiness, or material success they may have as the direct result of a strong will and sophisticated survival skills.

Throughout the 1990s, feminists challenged the codependency movement, suggesting that it was sexist. These researchers argued that women were far more likely than men to be considered codependent. In addition, the available definitions of codependency were inclined to pathologize the feminine identity and encouraged women to view themselves as sick in the context of significant relationships. Although these critiques of codependency have decreased in recent years, clinicians and researchers continue to question the therapeutic utility of codependency as a reliable means of characterizing and treating individuals who live with substance abusers (Calderwood & Rajesparam, 2014).

Finally, the characteristics associated with codependence are not exclusively unique to individuals who have been raised in families with a substance-abusing member. In fact, the criteria used to define codependency are applicable to many individuals, suggesting that the common thread might be that this cluster of characteristics is frequently seen in individuals who grow up in dysfunctional families. As any counselor is aware, this phenomenon is widespread, is not well defined, and may encompass the vast majority of clients seen in virtually any setting.

For all of these reasons, concerted efforts to study codependency waned. However, those individuals who live with a substance-abusing family member may struggle with issues of self-worth, self-esteem, identity, difficulty in relationships, and difficulty with boundaries. Those practitioners and educators who work with these individuals remain committed to the study of a helpful way to characterize this experience. To date, codependency remains the lone construct developed to capture this client population, and alongside the above-mentioned critiques, a sustained body of literature addressing codependency exists (Douglass, 2010).

Defining Codependency

In the 1980s, researchers working from a variety of theoretical orientations proposed different definitions for codependency (see Table 4). All of these definitions included a description of codependency as an illness of relationship that has its roots in an individual's primary and persistent relationship with someone who struggles with an SUD. The criteria used to define codependency fundamentally describe an inability to form and sustain relationships that are healthy and that are based on reciprocity and mutuality. The codependent individual has developed behavior patterns and perceptual disturbances that prohibit sound, reality-based methods of evaluating relationships using a balanced combination of external information and internal cues and feelings. It has been suggested that these disturbances are the result of relationships (primarily familial) with substance-abusing individuals in which the codependent person is forced to develop ways of relating that do not threaten this primary relationship with the substance-abusing individual (Dear, Roberts, & Lange, 2004).

In one of the earliest definitions of codependency, Robin Norwood (1985)—using an interpersonal framework—explained that the codependent person is an individual who has developed an unhealthy pattern of relating to others as a result of having been closely involved with a substance abuser. Anne Wilson Shaef (1986) proposed a more global definition of codependence as a systemic disease process that has its roots in the primary system where we reside and develop. As such, it is an illness that can be characterized as having origins in factors and relationships that reside outside of the codependent individual.

Table 4
Definitions of Codependency

Researcher	Definition's Salient Features
Black	There are three rules of families with a substance-abusing member: Don't talk. Don't trust. Don't feel.
Friel & Friel	Adherence to the dysfunctional rules of families with a substance-abusing member leads to identity disturbances within family members.
Edwards	Denial is the defining characteristic of codependence, leading to projective identification or splitting.
Larsen	Codependence is defined in terms of the specific roles that family members will assume that will dominate behavior in all relationships.
Norwood	Codependence is the result of a close relationship with a substance-abusing individual leading to the following intra-psychic symptoms: low self-esteem, a need to be needed, a strong urge to change and control others, and a willingness to suffer.
Wegscheider-Cruse	Codependence is a condition characterized by extreme dependence on a person or object, which leads to denial, compulsions, frozen feelings, low self-esteem, and stress-related medical conditions.
Whitfield	Codependence is a primary illness with a recognizable, diagnosable, and treatable set of symptoms and a chronic progressive prognosis.
Shaef	Shaef defined the "addictive process" as any substance or process we feel we have to lie about and relates this process to Freud's death instinct, as it is progressively death oriented.

Although there is certainly an interactional component between the individual and the environment, the inception of this disease has its basis in external forces beyond the control of the codependent.

There are a number of explanations for the process through which the interaction between the individual and the environment leads to codependency. Claudia Black (2001) suggested that within family systems organized around substance abuse, there are three consistent rules that pave the way for codependency: "Don't talk. Don't trust. Don't feel" (p. 9). Within a family system where these rules underlie family relationships, honest expression of authentic feelings is prohibited. When relationship patterns based on such rules become embedded and extend beyond relationships with family members, a codependent pattern of relating to the world ensues. In essence, these rules become embedded within the codependent person and become an organizing structure for future relationships. In addition, Black addressed the issue of denial as a central feature of codependency.

Edwards (2008) linked codependency to projective identification. Projective identification involves the substance abuser's projection of feelings that he or she is unable to access and process onto the codependent individual. What distinguishes projective identification from classic projection is the codependent individual's response to the projection. A codependent individual is more likely to assume the projected attributes than someone who is not struggling with codependency. In this way, the substance-abusing individual is successful at projecting the feelings not just onto the codependent individual, but actually into that person. For example, an individual with an SUD might relentlessly insist that the codependent person is highly controlling. In this case, the substance-abusing individual might insinuate that it is the codependent person's controlling nature that is responsible for the substance abuse issue. If, in reality, it is the substance abuser who is controlling and not the codependent, this would represent a case of classic projection—an individual projecting attributes onto another that are, in fact, characteristic of himself or herself. Projective identification in this case would occur if the codependent person assumes ownership of the attribute incorrectly assigned to him or her—in this case, a controlling nature—and willingly accepts this characterization of his or her behavior. Ultimately, both the substance-abusing individual and the codependent person agree that the attribute is most appropriately assigned to the codependent person. Cermak (1986) suggested that this swallowing whole of the other's projection is one of the clinical indications that a client is actually codependent, as the client will accept or at least wonder at his or her own culpability regarding the existence of the SUD. Because codependent people's own sense of self is diminished, their ability to discern reality is influenced such that they are sometimes easily manipulated. They are unable to achieve a clear interpretation of which attributes have been projected upon them by the substance-abusing individual and which truly belong to them.

Friel and Friel (2010) suggested that codependency involves overreacting to external events while ignoring internal cues and feelings. If untreated, these behavior patterns may develop into an addiction of sorts, with the codependent person experiencing a deep sense of an inability to alter unhealthy patterns. According to Friel and Friel's definition, codependent individuals have tremendous difficulty using internal cues and feelings to assess relationships. Having cut themselves off from these internal signals, they will tend to exaggerate external events and thus maintain a sense of hypervigilance, as they are not able to access any sense of personal power. They are forever at the mercy of the external world and feel ill equipped to bring an honest self-evaluation to situations and relationships.

Other definitions of codependence include expansions on the precise roles codependent people might assume as they navigate the world. These roles are formed on the basis of relationship tactics that have been assumed in order to maintain a primary relationship with a substance-abusing individual. Larsen (1985) was perhaps the first to characterize codependent people on the basis of predictable roles they might fill in a family with a substance-abusing member. Woitiz (1983) and others within the addictions field further developed and expanded these roles, which include the following previously mentioned roles: the enabler, the hero, the scapegoat, the lost child, and the mascot.

Charles Whitfield (1987), a medical doctor, defined codependency using a behavioral framework. In the medical tradition, Whitfield suggested that codependency is a primary condition with diagnosable and treatable symptoms and a chronic and progressive prognosis similar to that of an SUD. Wegscheider-Cruse (1989) operationally defined these symptoms. She described codependence as a condition that is characterized by extreme dependence (emotionally, socially, and sometimes physically) upon another person or an object. According to Wegscheider-Cruse, this dependence eventually becomes pathological and begins to infiltrate all of the codependent person's relationships. The specific characteristics associated with the disease of codependency include low self-esteem, frozen feelings, and stress-related medical disorders.

Cermak (1986) put forward the most thorough and comprehensive description of codependency to date by establishing diagnostic criteria for co-dependent personality disorder. Cermak initially defined codependency by stating that "the salient feature of codependency is continued investment of self-esteem in the ability to control feelings and behaviors, whether in oneself or others, in the face of adverse consequences" (p. 11). He went on to describe the codependent individual as someone with boundary distortions that include enmeshed relationships and an exaggerated sense of one's own responsibility to meet the needs of others while neglecting the meeting of one's own needs. In elaborating upon this definition, he went on to suggest that because codependence is composed of a recognizable pattern of personality traits predictably found within most members of chemically dependent families, specific diagnostic criteria were warranted. Thus, in 1986, Cermak presented the following set of diagnostic criteria for codependence and proposed it for inclusion within the *DSM-III*. Although it was not adopted for inclusion into the *DSM*, this framework is perhaps the most comprehensive and inclusive listing of characteristics associated with codependency and was considered and studied for many years after its initial presentation (Harkness, 2001).

Cermak's (1986) Proposed Diagnostic Criteria for Co-Dependent Personality Disorder

A. Continued investment of self-esteem in the ability to control both oneself and others in the face of serious adverse consequences.
B. Assumption of responsibility for meeting others' needs to the exclusion of acknowledging one's own.

C. Anxiety and boundary distortions around intimacy and separation.

D. Enmeshment in relationships with personality disordered, chemically dependent, other co-dependent, and/or impulse disordered individuals.

E. Three or more of the following:
1. Excessive reliance on denial
2. Constriction of emotions (with or without dramatic outbursts)
3. Depression
4. Hypervigilance
5. Compulsions
6. Anxiety
7. Substance abuse
8. Has been (or is) the victim or recurrent physical or sexual abuse
9. Stress-related medical illnesses
10. Has remained in a primary relationship with an active substance abuser for at least 2 years without seeking outside help (pp. 16–17).

Cermak additionally provided a distinction between what he referred to as primary codependence and secondary codependence that connect to the earlier discussion on developmental theory. In primary codependence, a child is subjected to a psychic wounding process throughout crucial developmental stages. In an unhealthy family system (e.g., one in which one or both parents have some level of SUD), the developing child receives a preponderance of conflicting, often destructive messages. This experience inhibits the development of an authentic self (Whitfield, 1987). In response, the child begins the process of negating and eventually destroying the true self, developing a codependent self to engage the world. This process leaves the child with a deep sense of emptiness and shame, as he or she becomes more and more convinced that if anyone got close to the true or authentic self, that person would certainly abandon him or her. Primary codependence is difficult to treat and has been characterized as a personality disorder. The dysfunction is deeply ingrained, as the individual develops unhealthy patterns of behavior beginning in early childhood.

Secondary codependence presents as a more reactionary pattern of unhealthy behaviors (Cermak, 1991). In this case, an otherwise healthy individual may begin to develop unhealthy behavior patterns in response to a relationship with a substance-abusing individual. Secondary codependence may be easier to treat in that the individual is more likely to have a healthy and solid core. The unique features associated with secondary codependence reside in the fact that these individuals will likely describe a childhood that has not been dominated by adults with SUD. Instead, for individuals presenting with secondary codependence issues, the relationships that have created the codependent behaviors will have emerged later in life, perhaps in late adolescence, early adulthood, or middle adulthood.

Finally, Cermak (1991) described the relationship between narcissism and codependency and suggested that this relationship is another defining characteristic of codependency. He proposed that codependent people are naturally attracted to and have a symbiotic relationship of sorts with individuals who have characteristics of narcissistic personality disorder. Because a narcissistic individual possesses personality traits that encompass a sense of grandiosity and entitlement, a codependent person is perhaps the perfect mate. Whereas codependent people are generally in search of methods by which they can channel their sense of self into another, narcissistic individuals are simultaneously in search of people who can support the grandiose self they have constructed. It is interesting that both personality types have at their core shame; it has been suggested that both disorders might best be characterized as having roots in a defense against shame. In addition, Glenn Gabbard (1993) suggested that there is a type of narcissism that is hypervigilant. The hypervigilant narcissistic individual is plagued by oversensitivity, which is also characteristic of the codependent person.

Case Example for Codependency
• • •

Colleen is a 26-year-old graduate student who reports "issues with relationships." She is currently in a relationship with a 30-year-old man, Sean; she has been with him for 3 years. He is talking about marriage, but she is ambivalent. Although she claims to love him and cannot imagine life without him, she is aware that there are issues that she is afraid might be more serious than she previously thought.

To be specific, Colleen reports that Sean "drinks a lot." When this issue is discussed more fully, she says that although Sean manages to hold down a good job and appears very high functioning, he rarely goes a day without consuming alcohol. He will typically have several drinks every evening—more on weekend evenings. In addition to her concerns regarding Sean's drinking, she reports that he is often emotionally distant. He does not like to "talk" when issues come up. In general, he simply tells Colleen to resolve things in whatever manner she would like. This situation has led to a pattern within the relationship in which Colleen takes care of virtually all of the activities of daily living. Finally, while Sean provides leeway and space in allowing Colleen to take charge of many of the activities of daily living, he can be controlling in other ways. For example, Colleen feels obligated to check in with Sean, even if she is going to be just a few minutes late in getting home. He is also very concerned with her appearance, often monitoring her diet and suggesting what she should wear. When the counselor inquires about how Colleen feels about Sean's behavior, she reports that historically she has always thought of it as normal. In fact, she likes taking care of him and pleasing him by looking good. However, with the recent talk of marriage, she has begun to question some of the relationship patterns that have taken hold.

Reflection

At this point in the counseling process, the counselor is likely to notice some codependent tendencies in Colleen. She appears to be a caretaker and has been fairly comfortable in what sounds like a somewhat controlling relationship. The counselor might want to explore Colleen's history in order to better understand how she developed her style of relating.

When Colleen begins to discuss her history, she reports that she is the oldest girl in a large family—she has five siblings. Her mother has an AUD. Although Colleen's mother was high functioning in many ways, Colleen spent her childhood feeling worthless and not quite good enough. Colleen goes on to describe taking on a parentified role in her family; she was responsible for covering for her mother on many occasions. In addition, Coleen reports being a perfectionist and always feeling that she needed to be successful in any endeavor she undertook, from running track, to getting good grades, to outperforming all of her colleagues at her job.

Coleen recalls knowing at some point in her early adolescence that something was not right. She rarely received any acknowledgment from her parents, even though she was a very good student and athlete. She can only recall being criticized. Of course, she does not remember her very early childhood, but she was the oldest of five children born within a 7-year span, and she does know that her mother was always overwhelmed. She learned early on that the best way to get any positive attention was to be helpful, to need little, and to work hard to manage the environment so that it would not be as stressful for her mother. She cannot recall ever breaking down or expressing anger or asking for anything throughout her childhood.

Implications for the Counselor

Colleen presents as a fairly typical codependent person. For as long as she can remember, it has been her role to take care of others. In fact, this role appears to have been a survival mechanism throughout her childhood. In addition, Colleen aptly learned to need nothing. She is very adept at identifying and meeting others' needs but cannot recall a time when she expressed her own.

In working with Colleen, it will be important to establish a safe and trusting relationship. If Colleen's mother drank alcoholically throughout Colleen's entire childhood, navigating important developmental stages was likely challenging for Colleen. The counselor will ultimately want to assist Colleen in analyzing her thinking, particularly regarding relationships. Colleen has established a sense of relationships based on her codependent childhood, and this pattern may be detrimental as she begins to consider something like marriage.

Discussion Questions

1. Identify some of the specific behaviors that indicate issues of codependency.
2. What issues might you want to explore if in fact you believe that codependency is at the root of Colleen's current ambivalence?
3. How might you assess Colleen for issues of codependency? What additional information might you want to gather?
4. What are other issues you might anticipate working on with Colleen?

Chapter 7

Emotional Consequences of Living With a Person With an SUD

The emotional consequences of living with an individual who has an SUD span both specific psychiatric diagnoses described in the *DSM-5* and other emotional struggles (Devine, 2013; Kelley et al., 2010; Slutske et al., 2008; see Table 5). As discussed previously, when SUD is present within a family, dysfunctional patterns of relating become the norm within that system. These patterns initially can, and do, serve as effective coping mechanisms for the individuals within the family. Members of such a family develop strategies for protecting themselves within the system that benefit them tremendously for the period of time that they are living with the substance-abusing individual. However, these same coping strategies that might work well within the isolated family system can become self-destructive when individuals attempt to use them in other settings (Klostermann et al., 2011).

As was also discussed previously, families with a substance-abusing member tend to organize themselves around denial, shame, and control. As a result, regardless of the role an individual family member might play—or the coping style he or she might adopt—that individual is (a) acting in response to maintaining denial and keeping the family secret, (b) protecting the family from the shame associated with the potential discovery of the secret, and (c) doing what feels necessary to control the environment in such a way that the family can maintain its

Table 5
Psychiatric and Emotional Consequences of Living With an Individual Struggling With an SUD

Disorder/Consequence	Description
Psychiatric Disorders	
Mood disorders	
Depression	Feelings of numbness; sad mood; loss of pleasure in life activities; problems with concentration or sleep
Anxiety	Excessive worrying; apprehension; fear; rumination; hypervigilance
Personality disorders	
Borderline personality disorder	Impairments in self-functioning and interpersonal functioning; negative affectivity
Covert narcissism	Impairments in self-functioning and interpersonal functioning; pathological personality traits
Other Emotional Consequences	
Learned helplessness	A feeling that one cannot effect change in what is happening to oneself
Dissociation	A psychic phenomenon whereby the individual splits the personality
Hypervigilance	Constantly scanning of the environment and relationships for signs of potential danger
Low self-esteem	A sense of worthlessness; a self-assessment that involves a sense of being "less than"

Note. SUD = substance use disorder.

dysfunctional form of homeostasis. As you might imagine, there is a price paid for making these kinds of adaptations and internalizing them. The internalized emotional responses that develop are often perceived as normal and even healthy by the individual, as they allow for survival in a dysfunctional environment. Unfortunately, even when the coping strategies that evolve as a result of these internalized emotional responses involve behaviors that are negatively affecting the individual, he or she is likely to continue using the patterns that have become automatic (Hussong et al., 2008; Klostermann et al., 2011; Love Longman, 2014). Therefore, the counselor should work with this client population to identify and work through the emotional consequences of living with an individual with an SUD. In this chapter, I explore some of the emotional issues likely to emerge for this population of clients as well as how the professional counselor might respond.

Psychiatric Disorders

Mood Disorders

Mood disorders represent a cluster of psychiatric disorders described in the *DSM-5*. As indicated by the name categorizing these particular disorders, they involve a disruption in an individual's mood that is not consistent with environmental or situational factors present within the individual's life. Instead, they are pervasive and persistent, regardless of the circumstances present for the individual. The most common mood disorders are depressive mood disorders and anxiety disorders. In fact, these disorders are the most widely studied psychiatric disorders, and they affect the lives of more individuals than any of the other disorders covered in the *DSM-5* (Young & Skorga, 2013). Despite this pervasiveness, the precise cause of these disorders remains elusive and is thought to include a combination of factors that span environmental conditions, resiliency, and biological and chemical predispositions.

There are several environmental conditions predictive of depression and anxiety that are common in families with a substance-abusing member, and both depressive and anxiety disorders have been linked to familial substance abuse (Dunn et al., 2002; Park & Schepp, 2014). For example, neglect has been shown to predict depressive mood disorder, and prolonged high levels of stress have been associated with an increased risk of developing an anxiety disorder (Nikulina, Widom, & Brzustowicz, 2012). As discussed earlier, both of these conditions are common in families with a substance-abusing member (see Table 6).

Depressive Mood Disorders

Researchers have shown a significant link between depression and living with an individual with an SUD (Kelley et al., 2010; Klostermann et al., 2011; Park & Schepp, 2014). In fact, even when other variables such as adverse childhood experiences other than exposure to substance abuse and lower socioeconomic status are controlled, adult children of substance abusers are significantly more likely to struggle with depression (Fuller-Thomson, Katz, Phan, Liddycoat, & Brennenstuhl, 2013). It is therefore important for counselors to possess a working knowledge of depression when working with this population of clients. Often, clients struggling with depression will report feelings of numbness or dissociation, sad mood, loss of pleasure in life activities, and problems with concentration or sleep.

According the *DSM-5*, major depressive disorder is defined as follows:

A. Five (or more) of the following symptoms have been present during the same 2-week period and represent a change from previous functioning; at least one of the symptoms is either (1) depressed mood or (2) loss of interest or pleasure.
Note: Do not include symptoms that are clearly attributable to another medical condition.
1. Depressed mood most of the day, nearly every day, as indicated by either subjective report (e.g., feels sad, empty, hopeless) or observation made by others (e.g., appears tearful). (*Note:* In children and adolescents, can be irritable mood.)

Table 6
Depression and Anxiety and Familial Substance Abuse

Psychiatric Disorder and Attributes of Families Affected by Substance Abuse	Psychological Response	Commonly Observed Disorder Indicators
Depression		
Neglect characterized by:	Significant abnormalities in neurotransmitters	Feelings of numbness or dissociation
• Preoccupation with substance use	Abnormal brain tissue	Sad mood
• Inability to meet individual needs	Smaller brain size	Loss of pleasure in life activities
• Limited attention to basic needs		Problems with sleep and concentration
Anxiety		
Stress characterized by:	Activation of HPA system	Excessive worrying
• Disorganized and chaotic	Release of cortisol	Apprehension
• Unpredictable	Release of neurotransmitters	Fear
• Prone to traumatic family events		Rumination
		Hypervigilance

Note. HPA = hypothalamic–pituitary–adrenal.

2. Markedly diminished interest or pleasure in all, or almost all, activities most of the day, nearly every day (as indicated by either subjective account or observation).
3. Significant weight loss when not dieting or weight gain (e.g., a change of more than 5% of body weight in a month), or decrease or increase in appetite nearly every day. (Note: In children, consider failure to make expected weight gain.)
4. Insomnia or hypersomnia nearly every day.
5. Psychomotor agitation or retardation nearly every day (observable by others, not merely subjective feelings of restlessness or being slowed down).
6. Fatigue or loss of energy.
7. Feelings of worthlessness or excessive or inappropriate guilt (which may be delusional) nearly every day (not merely self-reproach or guilt about being sick).
8. Diminished ability to think or concentrate, or indecisiveness, nearly every day (either by subjective account or as observed by others).
9. Recurrent thoughts of death (not just fear of dying), recurrent suicidal ideation without a specific plan, or a suicide attempt or a specific plan for committing suicide.
B. The symptoms cause clinically significant distress or impairment in social, occupational, or other important areas of functioning.
C. The episode is not attributable to the psychological effects of a substance or to another medical condition.
   Note: Criteria A–C represent a major depressive episode.

Note. From the *Diagnostic and Statistical Manual of Mental Disorders,* Fifth Edition (pp. 160–161), by American Psychiatric Association, 2013, Arlington, VA: American Psychiatric Association. Copyright 2013 by American Psychiatric Association. Reprinted with permission. All Rights Reserved.

Within the counseling profession, the root of depression was histori-cally thought to be environmental, and professional counselors worked with depressed clients within a developmental framework. Counselors relied heavily on treating depression using talk therapy as a method of revealing the underlying issues in a client's life that might be causing the depression. For individuals living in a family with a substance-abusing individual, counseling frequently included the processing of this experience as a means of treating the depression. Although this processing remains an important part of the treatment protocol for depressed clients who have lived or are currently living with an individual with an SUD, current scientific and medical research of depressive disorders suggests that the environmental circumstances originally thought to cause depression are sometimes directly linked to biological processes and mechanisms within the brain. An understanding of the neurobiological underpinnings of depression may help to explain the automatic responses typical for this client population and the powerful inclination to continue the use of dysfunctional coping strategies.

One relevant body of research suggests that a deficit of specific neurotransmitters explains depression (Ingram, Atchley, & Segal, 2011). From this perspective, it is postulated that depressed in-dividuals may possess lower synaptic levels of the neurotransmit-ters serotonin, dopamine, or norepinephrine. In other words, the specific synapses (the mechanisms through which neurons in the brain speak to each other) charged with regulating the transmis-sion of serotonin, dopamine, or norepinephrine are malfunctioning (Blier, 2013).

Other research examining the role of neuroscience on psy-chiatric disorders has found that the development of lower syn-aptic levels of these critical neurotransmitters has been linked to experiences known to be typical for individuals living with a family member who has an SUD. For example, the association between neglect and the development of depressive disorders has been established (Nutt, 2008; Sperry & Widom, 2013). In fact, scientists interested in the impact of neglect on both behavior and the brain have reported findings that are quite staggering. In one study (Matsumoto, Pinna, Puia, Guidotti, & Costa, 2005), researchers isolated one group of mice and compared them with a group that had not been isolated. The mice that were isolated showed significant brain abnormalities, specifically in the neu-rotransmitters. In a related study, researchers isolated 21-day-old mice for 2 weeks and then returned them to the larger group. When the mice reached adolescence, the researchers compared the brains and the behavior of the mice that had been isolated for the 2-week period with the mice that had never been isolated. The mice isolated for only 2 weeks of their lives were antisocial, showed deficits in memory, and had significantly abnormal brain tissue. Matsumoto et al. (2005) concluded that isolation (i.e., neglect) had a profound impact on brain development, and that the neglected mice engaged in behaviors associated with depression when they reached adolescence.

These studies have been extended to several larger-scale studies involving tracking children who began their lives in an orphanage. The findings associated with these studies revealed that children who spent their first 2 years in the orphanage displayed higher levels of depression and smaller brain sizes than children not raised in an orphanage. The depressive disorders persisted, regardless of whether the children were later adopted (Yendork & Somhlaba, 2014). These researchers inferred that neglect in very early childhood seemed to predict depression later in life.

All of this research is relevant for counselors working with individuals who have lived with a substance-abusing family member. To be specific, these studies point to the changes that can occur within the brain as a result of neglect. Having established that families with a substance-abusing member tend to organize around the addiction, neglect is a logical consequence. In such families, neglect can take a variety of forms. However, it is generally pervasive, as the individual members of these families rarely have their needs met in a consistent, healthy manner. The ongoing and pervasive chaos characteristic of families with a substance-abusing member prohibit the environmental conditions necessary to avoid the consequences of neglect and isolation (Love Longman, 2014). These environmental circumstances are linked to changes in the brain that are associated with depressive symptoms. Thus, the powerful inclinations to behave in ways that reinforce depressive symptomatology can be partially explained as biochemical and thus may be more difficult to treat using only talk therapy. For the professional counselor, it is important to assess depressive symptoms with clients who have lived with substance-abusing family members. In the event that the client and the counselor determine that the depressive symptomatology is not responding to talk therapy, a psychiatric consult may be warranted. Although the counselor can continue using talk therapy with such a client, a psychiatric assessment to determine the severity and chronicity of the depressive symptoms is sometimes necessary.

Case Example for Depressive Disorders

Juan, a 32-year-old Mexican American man, originally comes into counseling because he is unhappy in his job. Although he presents with a somewhat flat affect, he reports not feeling depressed. The counselor suspects that more is going on with Juan than he is reporting, but she is unable to get him to engage with material at a deeper level. Juan comes for about six sessions and then reports feeling better and decides to terminate the counseling.

About a year later, Juan calls the counselor again to inquire if she ever deals with more than career issues, that is, if she also deals with emotional content. Of course the counselor is pleased to report that she does, in fact, do this kind of work and schedules an appointment with Juan.

Reflection

In reflecting on this case up to this point, the counselor might be glad that Juan is expressing interest in working on emotional issues. In addition, the counselor is likely to understand that this work might be difficult for Juan. On the basis of Juan's reluctance to address emotional content a year earlier, it might be that he has come to this decision slowly. Therefore, working with Juan to create a safe therapeutic relationship is likely to be an initial goal of counseling.

Juan and the counselor begin to work in earnest, and eventually Juan discloses that his childhood was traumatic. However, throughout the telling of the story, Juan is very careful to disclose events and information in a way that defends the trauma. For example, when Juan shares that his alcoholic mother was often asleep when he returned home from school, he quickly adds, "But she had physical issues as well," and that "It was really OK because by the time [he] can remember this as the pattern, [he] was old enough to watch [his] two younger brothers until she awoke."

Over time, as trust between the counselor and Juan continues to develop, he begins to relax in his telling of his story. As Juan continues to process some of the feelings he had previously denied, he begins to explore how denial and control have dictated so much of his emotional life. For example, Juan has clearly been denying the extent to which his mother's drinking affected his earlier development. In order to maintain his denial, Juan has forcefully controlled his emotional reactions, especially those associated with the feelings of loss this situation elicited. As he begins to process these feelings of loss, Juan finds that his sadness deepens. It seems that the more he allows himself full access to some of these feelings, the sadder he becomes. He reports being extremely tired much of the time and having trouble finding pleasure or feeling joy. In addition, it is difficult for Juan to feel much passion. He describes himself as somewhat numb.

As the counseling sessions continue, Juan begins to share his recent struggles with relationships. He describes himself as unable to maintain an intimate relationship and shares that he had recently met someone new. He reports that he is determined "not to screw this one up." Although he does not initially link this life event with his background, he does describe that he sometimes feels like his sadness and fear of intimacy have been a part of his life for as long as he could remember, and he acknowledges that these feelings often have preceded the ending of relationships. Juan expresses his profound disappointment in himself and concludes that he must be defective in some way. He sees this "defectiveness" as the essential reason for his struggles.

As Juan continues to explore the reality of his childhood, both he and his counselor become aware of how pervasively his depressed mood is affecting his current life. They agree that Juan should have a psychiatric consult and that he should simultaneously continue counseling.

Implications for the Counselor

In working with any client who has lived with an individual with an SUD, building rapport is essential and may take longer than with other clients. When a client has learned to deny reality and this denial becomes deeply internalized, the client is likely to generalize the denial to include altering present-day realities that feel familiar in any way. In addition, this denial is likely to be linked with shame. Therefore, even when the client is more able to access the truth, this internalized shame is very likely to push the client toward moving back to a state of denial. Shame is a very powerful force and an extremely uncomfortable feeling. For many individuals who have internalized shame, any perception of judgment can cause them to shut down. They live with an ongoing fear that if they are truly revealed, they will certainly be abandoned. Therefore, in working with these clients, it is critically important for the counselor to be patient, build rapport, build trust, and maintain a completely nonjudgmental stance.

In working with any client who is exhibiting signs of a depressive mood disorder, it is important to establish whether this diagnosis is a possibility. If, in fact, a counselor does determine that a client's depression is affecting his or her life in adverse ways that do not seem to be responding to talk therapy, a referral for a psychiatric evaluation should be made. A psychiatrist can determine whether medication is indicated; such medication should be considered in the event that talk therapy is not promoting sufficient positive outcomes for the client.

In addition, cognitive behavior therapy has been shown to be effective with depressed people. Chapter 11 discusses how to use this form of treatment with clients affected by a family member's SUD.

Discussion Questions

1. Why do you imagine that the establishment of trust might be especially significant for clients who have lived with a family member with an SUD? How do you see this playing out with Juan?
2. How would you proceed with Juan in order to determine if he is, in fact, struggling with a depressive or anxiety disorder?

3. Do you think that Juan's depressed mood is linked to his earlier experience of being raised by a mother who has an AUD? Why or why not?

Anxiety Disorders

Anxiety is the most commonly diagnosed emotional disorder. In the United States, it is estimated that 18% of all adults will struggle with an anxiety disorder during the course of their lifetime (Seif, 2014). In addition, it has been reported that the comorbidity of anxiety and depression is 58%; in fact, the two disorders share symptomatology. For both disorders, affected individuals tend to report a sad mood and a decrease in the experience of pleasure within their lives. In addition, both groups often report irritability, agitation, and tension. The *DSM-5* describes a number of anxiety disorders, including generalized anxiety disorder, panic disorder and agoraphobia, social anxiety disorder, and specific phobias. In the case of anxiety, clients will often report excessive worrying, apprehension, fear, rumination, and hypervigilance.

Scientists have discerned a fairly sophisticated understanding of the neurological mechanisms contributing to anxiety (Seif, 2014). In particular, the human body's physiological response to stress is well understood. When people are exposed to stress, the hypothalamic–pituitary–adrenal (HPA) system is automatically activated. When this activation occurs, the body releases specific hormones, including cortisol. Because cortisol is a hormone that plays a large role in organizing systems throughout the body—including circulation, respiration, and the immune system—these systems are directly affected in a stress response. At the same time that the HPA system is releasing stress hormones, it releases specific neurotransmitters, including dopamine, norepinephrine, and adrenaline. The combination of these automatic physiological responses to stress then affect systems throughout the body. Breathing becomes more rapid, heart rate is increased, and portions of the immune system are depressed (Yudofsky, 2012).

When an anxiety disorder is present for an individual, this physiological response—designed to allow an individual short-term strength, speed, and concentration in the face of real danger—can be activated in response to common life events. In addition, the body's response to the physiological stress reaction is intended to be "fight or flight." In other words, our body prepares to either fight a predator or run. In both cases, a physiological discharge of the excess hormones occurs. An individual with an anxiety disorder, on the other hand, does not necessarily experience the physical release of stress hormones. Instead, the body tends to hold the stress (Kunimatsu & Marsee, 2012).

The brain pathways developed in response to ongoing stress create a vulnerability for developing anxiety disorders (Lang,

McTeague, & Bradley, 2014). This vulnerability may explain why anxiety disorders are prevalent among children of substance abusers (Devine, 2013), as these children are often undergoing significant brain development during a time of high stress. Individuals who experience high levels of ongoing stress during the time that critical brain circuitry is developing can become "hard wired" in ways that predispose them to increased levels of anxiety. The physiological response to stimuli that trigger an anxious response can become automatic.

Understanding the neuroscience associated with the development of anxiety disorders is important. However, the professional counselor's job is to work directly with the client's environmental triggers as well as his or her thoughts associated with high levels of anxiety. In the case of clients who live or have lived with an individual with an SUD, some developmental tasks have likely been tackled within an environment affected by the substance use. Depending on the age of the individual and the developmental tasks encountered, the type and severity of a potential anxiety disorder will likely vary.

In addition to an increased vulnerability to anxiety disorders, clients exposed to trauma or substance abuse are at increased risk for posttraumatic stress disorder (PTSD; Haller, 2013; Kachadourian, Pilver, & Potenza, 2014; Shepherd & Wild, 2014). Listed as an anxiety disorder in the *DSM-IV*, PTSD is now considered a trauma- and stressor-related disorder (APA, 2013). In particular, a client who was raised by an individual with an SUD (especially where that individual was the primary caretaker during the very early developmental stages) may present with significant PTSD. PTSD is described as a psychiatric disorder that develops in response to one or more traumatic events. The characteristics of PTSD include reoccurring flashbacks of the incident, avoidance of memories of the event, numbing emotional response to the event, and hyperarousal after the occurrence of the event.

In the case of individuals who live with a family member with an SUD, PTSD can occur as a response to any number of traumatic events experienced by or witnessed by the individual. Because of the chaotic nature and inconsistency characteristic of these families, individual members are at an increased risk of experiencing trauma. Depending on factors such as the severity of the trauma, the age at which an individual experienced the trauma, and the consistency of trauma-inducing events, clients who have lived with a substance-abusing family member may present with PTSD symptomatology or with full-blown PTSD (Haller, 2013).

As with depressive mood disorders, anxiety disorders may require psychiatric intervention. As a counselor works with an individual who presents with anxiety, it is important to monitor symptoms and continuously assess the extent to which these symptoms are interfering with functioning for the client. In the event that the counselor and the client conclude that the level of anxiety is persistently affecting the individual's overall psychological well-being, a psychiatric evaluation should be considered.

Case Example for Anxiety Disorders
• • •

Keith, a 47-year-old Caucasian man, has come for counseling to deal with what he refers to as his "minor panic attacks." Keith describes himself as a type A person who has always been a perfectionist. He is driven and has very high standards for himself.

At present, Keith is finding it more difficult to manage his anxiety. He reports that he used to be able to simply push through the discomfort, but he has recently had experiences where he felt paralyzed by the anxiety. He is confused, as he is unable to make sense of his feelings. Keith describes his life as pretty perfect. He claims to have a solid, loving marriage of 18 years and two happy, well-adjusted children. He has a job that he loves and feels successful in and feels that he has a close and extensive support system.

Reflection

The counselor might note that Keith's fairly consistent feelings of anxiety do not fit with his description of his life circumstances. This is an area that the counselor might wish to explore, as there is likely more to this picture than has been revealed thus far. The counselor might proceed by attempting to clarify the connection between the feelings of anxiety Keith describes and any life circumstances or experiences that might shed light on these feelings.

As the counseling progresses, Keith begins to share information about his earlier life. Keith grew up in a strict upper-middle-class family. His father worked as a midlevel executive for a large corporation, and his mother stayed home. Keith was the youngest of four children: Brett, 11 years older than Keith; Stacy, 8 years older than Keith; and Michael, 6 years older than Keith. As the youngest child, and given the age differences between himself and his siblings, Keith often felt isolated as a child. He describes feeling invisible much of the time.

Keith remembers that when he was about 6, his brother Brett began to "have problems." Although at this age, Keith was unclear as to the nature of those problems, by the time he was 9, he was very aware that his brother Brett was a drug addict. Keith's memories of this time are filled with sadness and anxiety. He recalls a lot of screaming, threatening, crying, and general chaos at home. Keith tried to spend as much time as he could away from home, but he never felt safe and was always unsure of what he would return to when he did go home.

When the counselor explored what kinds of supports Keith might have used during this time, he found that there were virtually none. Keith described that he knew that Brett's addiction was a huge secret and that he was not to divulge this situation to anyone. In fact, to this day, he has rarely spoken of those years and has only shared this part of his past with his wife. As a child, Keith made the decision to be perfect. He describes knowing that he would never put his parents through this kind of ordeal again. In addition, being perfect and successful gave Keith a focus and direction and allowed him to compartmentalize and avoid dealing with the reality of his life.

Recently, however, Keith is unable to use these same coping strategies to ignore his anxiety. In fact, he is finding that trying to be perfect is creating additional stress now. Keith's children are both adolescents and thus unpredictable, and he has recently transitioned in his job to assume greater responsibility. In both his personal and professional life, Keith is currently unable to either control or even predict events. He describes that when this happens and he is thrown in any way, his anxiety skyrockets and he feels frozen.

Implications for the Counselor

Keith is describing debilitating anxiety that exemplifies PTSD. In situations where he experiences a loss of control or perhaps in circumstances that are reminiscent of his childhood experiences of living with a family member with an SUD (e.g., his children reaching adolescence), the anxious reaction seems to be triggered. Even though these current circumstances may not be traumatic or even particularly worrisome, they trigger a response that is linked to an earlier event that may have contained similar features or elements. For example, if Keith comes home to a fight between his wife and one of his adolescent children regarding curfew, his internal reaction to this might mimic a panic attack, when in fact the actual event is not traumatic or even highly emotionally laden.

As discussed earlier, PTSD is sometimes linked to familial substance abuse. When an individual lives for a period of time in an environment where chaos and unpredictability are the norm, anxiety can easily be triggered. With no outlet for the anxious response, a child in particular is likely to internalize this experience. Later, when events are similar in nature to the original event, this anxiety can be triggered even when this response does not fit the current circumstance.

In terms of treatment, cognitive behavioral techniques can be very effective with anxiety. (Again, these are covered in more detail later in this book.) In addition, the counselor must assess whether a psychiatric examination is indicated. In the event that the client's anxiety is significantly affecting his or her psychological well-being, it is likely that a psychiatric consultation makes sense.

Discussion Questions

1. How might you help Keith make the connections between his earlier experience and his current-day struggles with anxiety?
2. What role might you assume denial and shame are playing in this case?
3. What are some of the counseling goals you might consider in working with Keith?
4. Do you think it is important for Keith to get in touch with and process feelings he may have avoided? Why or why not?
5. How would you determine if a psychiatric consultation is indicated?

Personality Disorders

Personality disorders are characterized by the fundamental nature of the impairment. In essence, individuals with a personality disorder will exhibit pathological personality traits. Unlike the mood disorders discussed previously, a personality disorder is likely to permeate identity as well as interpersonal relationships for the diagnosed individual. Thus, personality disorders tend to affect people's day-to-day functioning as well as their ability to maintain an identity that allows them to function well in the context of all of the various relationships a typical adult is likely to encounter (APA, 2013).

The particular personality disorders linked to clients who have lived with an individual with an SUD (particularly those raised by a substance abuser) are borderline personality disorder (BPD) and covert narcissism. These disorders are serious and likely to involve time and intensive work, as they are resistant to change and involve a depth of entanglement. For the professional counselor, an individual with a personality disorder represents a client who is likely to require long-term counseling and the use of specific interventions that have been shown to effect positive change for this client population (Dixon-Gordon, Turner, & Chapman, 2011).

Borderline Personality Disorder

According to the *DSM-5* (APA, 2013, p. 663), the following criteria are used to diagnose BPD:

> A pervasive pattern of instability of interpersonal relationships, self-image, and affects, and marked impulsivity, beginning by early adulthood and present in a variety of contexts, as indicated by five (or more) of the following:
>
> 1. Frantic efforts to avoid real or imagined abandonment. (*Note:* Do not include suicidal or self-mutilating behavior covered in Criterion 5.)
> 2. A pattern of unstable and intense interpersonal relationships characterized by alternating between extremes of idealization and devaluation.
> 3. Identity disturbance: markedly and persistently unstable self-image or sense of self.

4. Impulsivity in at least two areas that are potentially self-damaging (e.g., spending, sex, substance abuse, reckless driving, binge eating). (*Note:* Do not include suicidal or self-mutilating behavior covered in Criterion 5.)
5. Recurrent suicidal behavior, gestures, or threats, or self-mutilating behavior.
6. Affective instability due to a marked reactivity of mood (e.g., intense episodic dysphoria, irritability, or anxiety usually lasting a few hours and only rarely more than a few days).
7. Chronic feelings of emptiness.
8. Inappropriate intense anger or difficulty controlling anger (e.g., frequent displays of temper, constant anger, recurrent physical fights).
9. Transient, stress-related paranoid ideation or severe dissociative symptoms.

Note. From the *Diagnostic and Statistical Manual of Mental Disorders,* Fifth Edition (p. 663), by American Psychiatric Association, 2013, Arlington, VA: American Psychiatric Association. Copyright 2013 by American Psychiatric Association. Reprinted with permission. All Rights Reserved.

SUD has been linked to BPD (Sansone & Sansone, 2011). In addition, emotional abuse in childhood has been shown to result in difficulties with emotional regulation throughout life (Kuo, Khoury, Metcalf, Fitzpatrick, & Goodwill, 2014), and early childhood trauma has been shown to predict BPD (Fernando et al., 2014; van Dijke, Ford, van Son, Frank, & van der Hart, 2013). Therefore, the chaotic and unpredictable environment characteristic of a home in which a family member has an SUD sets the stage for the early experiences shown to predict BPD. In the case of BPD, the risk is much greater for children of substance abusers than it might be for individuals who lived their early childhood years in a more predictable and less traumatic environment and came to live with a substance abuser later in life. As discussed previously, the earliest developmental stages represent a time of tremendous impact. Excessive trauma and chaos during these vulnerable developmental times is likely to place individuals at risk for significant issues throughout subsequent developmental stages. Finally, the denial and shame so often associated with families with a substance-abusing member have been shown to lead to feelings of emptiness and issues with self-image, features associated with BPD (Hinrichs, DeFife, & Westen, 2011).

Case Example for BPD
• • •

Judith, a 22-year-old Caucasian female, has come for counseling following a recent hospitalization for depression and suicidal ideation. She was referred to the counselor by the hospital social worker. While hospitalized, Judith was prescribed Lexapro for depression and diazepam for anxiety and had a follow-up visit scheduled with a local psychiatrist.

During her first session, Judith shares that she only wound up hospitalized because her mother was hysterical and loved drama.

However, Judith also shares several text conversations she had with her mother prior to her hospitalization, in which she clearly articulated her desire to end her life and specified a method for doing so. When this discrepancy between her characterization of her mother as hysterical and her own words within the text messages is brought to Judith's attention, she states, "Oh, she knew I didn't mean that."

Throughout the course of the first session, Judith vacillates between talking about her mother and talking about the various staff at the hospital. In each description of a particular individual, Judith focuses on what that person has done to victimize her. Although the counselor attempts throughout the session to bring the discussion back to Judith, it remains difficult to keep the focus on the client, as she continues to talk about others who are ultimately responsible for her behavior. When the counselor attempts to clarify with Judith her goals for counseling, Judith is vague and indicates that she only wants these other people to respond as she thinks they should.

Reflection

To this point, the counseling process with Judith has likely been challenging for the counselor. On the basis of Judith's participation in the process thus far, the counselor is not likely to have an easy time establishing a therapeutic alliance with Judith, as a genuine connection appears difficult in this case. Thus far, Judith has been unable to demonstrate a consistent, mature self-image that includes assuming responsibility within her relationships.

In subsequent sessions, Judith continues to divert the focus from herself and onto others in her life. Although the sessions are somewhat disjointed, Judith does begin to disclose the role that drugs and alcohol have played in her family of origin. Judith describes her mother as a "typical codependent." She claims that her mother was the child of an alcoholic mother and brought her codependence into her parenting role. In addition, Judith characterizes her father as a major cocaine addict. Her father works as a financial analyst and makes a very good living. Judith reports that despite her father's high income, their family always seemed to be struggling to make ends meet. She states that her mother has always confided in her regarding her father's drug use, and that this makes her feel important. Judith also describes tremendous inconsistencies in her home life. Her mother would be friendly (i.e., she would confide in Judith and treat her as a personal friend) one day and full of rage the next day. They would go on a family outing to a park and have a wonderful day, and her parents would engage in a violent fight that night. These kinds of experiences were typical for Judith throughout her childhood.

When the counselor attempts to stay with this content within counseling sessions, Judith quickly moves to other topics, inevitably involving another individual in her life who has disappointed her in some manner. In addition, she continues to vacillate from fury to sadness as she recalls her childhood. Judith shares that her coping strategies throughout her adolescent years included risk taking. She claims that she was sexually promiscuous and was then frequently disappointed by the "jerks" who used her. She reports that she would usually respond to this rejection by repeatedly e-mailing the individual who betrayed her, threatening to expose him for the person she knew him to be. Judith would then become morose and depressed until she met someone new.

Although progress remains slow, the counselor stays with Judith, attempting to meet her where she is, while simultaneously gently pushing her to acknowledge and work with reality. Judith continues to resist the counselor's efforts in this regard but does continue with counseling. Eventually, Judith and the counselor reach the place where they began to discuss the possibility of BPD as a possible diagnosis. Once this point had been reached and the counselor has been able to help Judith accept this possibility, specific strategies and techniques are incorporated into the counseling to specifically address this issue.

Implications for the Counselor

This particular case is extremely difficult. When a counselor begins to consider BPD as a possible diagnosis, it is likely that the case will be challenging. Judith is experiencing tremendous difficulty in allowing the focus of the counseling to be directly on her. At the same time, Judith expresses neediness and a desire to be completely heard and understood, conveying her insistence that others attend directly to her needs. In addition, her mood has vacillated throughout the counseling process, without a predictable pattern.

Although the basic counseling skills, as well as the use of varying cognitive strategies, can prove beneficial with this client population, dialectical behavioral therapy (DBT) has been shown to be particularly effective in working with individuals with BPD (Swales, Heard, & Williams, 2000). Because of the pervasive and intense nature of this disorder, traditional forms of talk psychotherapy alone do not generally lead to sustained changes for the client diagnosed with BPD. Instead, a more effective approach with these clients is to use more structured interventions that provide clients with a precise set of skills that can be used to manage the disorder . Some of these particular treatment techniques, including DBT, require specific training.

Discussion Questions

1. Would you consider a diagnosis of BPD to be appropriate in the case of Judith? Why or why not? What behaviors support or refute this diagnosis?

2. How are Judith's symptoms related to her childhood experiences of growing up with a father addicted to cocaine?
3. What strategies or interventions would you consider using in counseling Judith? How would you determine if more a more targeted treatment approach made sense?

Covert Narcissism

Another personality disorder often linked with substance use and abuse is a form of narcissistic personality disorder referred to as *covert narcissism*. In the case of an individual living with a family member struggling with an SUD, narcissistic tendencies are likely to be covert. According to the *DSM-5* (APA, 2013, pp. 669–670), the criteria for a narcissistic personality disorder are as follows:

> A pervasive pattern of grandiosity (in fantasy or behavior), need for admiration, and lack of empathy, beginning by early adulthood and present in a variety of contexts, as indicated by five (or more) of the following:
>
> 1. Has a grandiose sense of self-importance (e.g., exaggerates achievements and talents, expects to be recognized as superior without commensurate achievements).
> 2. Is preoccupied with fantasies of unlimited success, power, brilliance, beauty, or ideal love.
> 3. Believes that he or she is "special" and unique and can only be understood by, or should associate with, other special or high-status people (or institutions).
> 4. Requires excessive admiration.
> 5. Has a sense of entitlement (i.e., unreasonable expectations of especially favorable treatment or automatic compliance with his or her expectations).
> 6. Is interpersonally exploitative (i.e., takes advantage of others to achieve his or her own ends).
> 7. Lacks empathy: is unwilling to recognize or identify with the feelings and needs of others.
> 8. Is often envious of others or believes that others are envious of him or her.
> 9. Shows arrogant, haughty behaviors or attitudes.

Note. From the *Diagnostic and Statistical Manual of Mental Disorders,* Fifth Edition (pp. 669–670), by American Psychiatric Association, 2013, Arlington, VA: American Psychiatric Association. Copyright 2013 by American Psychiatric Association. Reprinted with permission. All Rights Reserved.

Although these criteria suggest overt displays of behaviors associated with this disorder, this manifestation is not always the case. Cooper (1998) originally described covert narcissism as being characterized by fantasies that include grandiose expectations and entitlement. These feelings are often manifested in high levels of worrying, defensiveness, and hostility. In contrast to the overt narcissist, however, the covert narcissist is not likely to express these fantasies. In fact, the covert narcissist is likely to carry guilt associated with the desires these fantasies elicit. For example, a covert narcissist might feel entitled to a lavish lifestyle. At the same time, he or she is likely to experience a deep sense of unworthiness, leading to guilt regarding his or her lifestyle fantasy. Cooper suggested that for the covert narcissist, the superego accurately assesses that the fantasies related to grandiosity are self-centered and support a desire for high levels of recognition and power. However, in doing its job, the superego simultaneously imposes a harsh, critical judgment of these thoughts. In other words, the superego works to support the cycle of entitlement–unworthiness–guilt.

Like the overt narcissist, the covert narcissist is likely to harbor intense anger. However, this anger is rarely expressed, as it violates the inner conscience that deems these thoughts and feelings unacceptable. Therefore, the covert narcissist is likely to internalize his or her anger and engage in high levels of self-degradation.

Covert narcissism has been linked to codependency, suggesting that individuals who live with a substance-abusing family member may be at an increased risk of struggling with this disorder (McDonald, 2013; Reyome, Ward, & Witklewitz, 2010). To be specific, clients identified as codependent displayed higher levels of rejection sensitivity, attachments to painful relationships, and shame-proneness (Wells, Hill, Brack, & Firestone, 2006). Each of these traits is characteristic of covert narcissism.

Identifying covert narcissism is difficult for counselors, as many of the traits associated with the disorder are also associated with other issues, which confounds the diagnostic process. For example, covert narcissism can initially mimic issues like low self-esteem or low self-worth. It is very likely that the covert narcissist will begin the therapeutic process by describing the situations that led him or her into counseling from a stance of self-deprecation. The counselor can easily interpret this self-deprecation as an issue related to a diminished sense of worthiness. However, over time, the covert narcissist will begin to reveal immature grandiose expectations. From a developmental perspective, it is typical for adolescents to possess a level of narcissism revealed in their descriptions and fantasies about what they will be able achieve (e.g., fame and fortune). However, it is expected that these fantasies will begin to temper through young and middle adulthood. This is not to say that an adult cannot possess goals that include fame and fortune. However, for a more healthy client, these expectations will continue to adapt to whatever realties exist for that individual. In addition, as individuals mature into adulthood, it is expected that goals and desires will continue to align more closely with the individual's sense of self-efficacy. In other words, adults are expected to see themselves clearly with regard to what they want and what they know they can do. In the case of covert narcissists, the likelihood is that they will possess a low level of self-efficacy. They are likely to see themselves as unable to achieve their goals. They often lack the confidence to attempt new ventures or even to follow a known path to the next level. At the same time, they will harbor grandiose fantasies that their psyche believes they deserve and anger at the fact that these fantasies have not been realized.

Case Example for Covert Narcissism

Audra is a 52-year-old African American woman who has come for counseling because of a sense of increasing emptiness and the feeling that nobody ever gets her. She reports that she is considering divorcing her second husband, Leon. Audra states that she is bored and feels unappreciated: She does not understand why Leon does not treat her in the same way he used to.

Her first marriage to Clint ended after 9 years. Audra describes that marriage as difficult. She reports that she never felt heard or understood by Clint, and that his expectations were not consistent with what she felt was reasonable. They tried couples counseling, but Audra reports that the counselor was biased and unable to see her point of view. Audra reports that she probably stayed married longer than she should have because they had two children.

Audra married Leon within a year of her divorce from Clint. She reports that the beginning of the relationship was wonderful; she felt that she had found her soul mate. However, recently, she feels disconnected from Leon, reporting that he cannot understand her either and does not show the unwavering interest in her that she received previously. Although she appears enraged at Leon about this situation, she expresses that it simply confirms that she is inadequate and unable to "keep a man." She claims that she knows that she deserves more, but she simultaneously suggests that she is so defective that she is sure she will never get what she deserves.

In talking about her children, Audra shares that Bryan, age 17, has always been a top student and successful athlete. However, he is now showing signs of anxiety and depression. Audra finds this very disturbing because she believes that it is proof that she has been an inadequate parent. Emma, age 14, is beginning to isolate, spending most of her time at home in her room and refusing to discuss even the most mundane aspects of her life with her mother. Audra used to feel that Emma and she were more like "best friends" than mother and daughter. She now feels rejected and horrible about herself in response to Emma's disinterest in sharing the intimate details of her current life.

Reflection

In working with Audra, the counselor is likely to begin to see a pattern emerging that reflects Audra's repeated disappointment in the relationships most important to her. These disappointments suggest an externalization of the source of her unhappiness: The reason she is distressed is entirely attributable to the behavior of others. At the same time, Audra's true focus is entirely on herself. She simultaneously sees herself as a victim and feels she is deserving of more. She also seems unable to be realistic in her relationships. For example, Audra expresses disappointment in her current relationship with her daughter without considering her daughter's developmental needs.

In addition, a pattern of self-degradation has emerged that Audra is able to reinforce with each perceived rejection in her life. Audra appears to see her disappointments as inevitable and completely outside of her control.

As Audra begins to discuss her childhood, she describes multiple traumatic events that primarily revolved around her mother's alcoholism. Audra cannot remember a time when her mother was not drinking, and she describes life in her childhood home as a roller coaster. Audra never knew what she would return to at the end of each school day, and she remembers horrific fights and scenes during which her parents would scream and shout and sometime throw things. However, Audra was always very aware of the importance of keeping the family secret. Her father was a minister in a large local Baptist church, and her family was expected to behave appropriately at all times. Therefore, Audra was very careful never to speak of the issues going on at home with anyone. She attempted to speak directly to her parents instead. She reports that she tried "millions of times" to talk to her parents about how she was feeling. However, whenever she attempted to address her fears with either parent, she was told to stop making such a big deal out of everything. They would explain that fighting is normal and her mother does not drink more than other adults. Audra recalls that after these discussions she questioned her own sanity and would inevitably decide that she must be crazy or at least exaggerating.

Implications for the Counselor

In working with a client like Audra, it is important to understand the depth of her issues. The emerging patterns indicate a pervasive condition that appears to engulf all of her most important relationships. What the counselor sees is the combination of entitlement and self-degradation indicative of covert narcissism. In addition, Audra reports slights, insults, and expectations that the counselor might expect to hear from an adolescent client. At the same time, Audra reports a persistent sense of self-loathing.

Although trust building and establishing a working rapport will be essential in working with Audra, a more directive and specific approach (e.g., DBT) is likely to be necessary in order to have an impact on Audra's thinking and behavior. If, in fact, Audra is struggling with covert narcissism, the counselor is dealing with a personality disorder. Personality disorders, by definition, are pervasive and generally require specific treatments in order to facilitate changes that can truly affect the client's quality of life.

Discussion Questions

1. Do you agree that Audra might be struggling with covert narcissism? Why or why not? What are the behaviors and thoughts that support your stand?
2. How might you connect Audra's history of living with an alcoholic parent to both her current-day issues and covert narcissism?

Other Emotional Consequences of Living With a Substance Abuser

Learned Helplessness

Learned helplessness refers to an internalized belief that one cannot change or affect what happens to one in life. Both uncontrollable outcomes and early trauma have been found to trigger learned helplessness. Although the initial event that triggers a sense of learned helplessness is likely to be real, the learned helplessness response is often generalized. Thus, individuals who struggle with a sense of learned helplessness fail to take advantage of opportunities to regain control, well after the trauma-inducing experience has occurred. Therefore, decisions regarding their ability to control various aspects of their lives can forever be formed on the basis of a small sample of past experiences (Teodorescu & Erev, 2014).

Learned helplessness has been linked to major depressive disorder and PTSD. In fact, this connection has been made both with the observable characteristics of these conditions and with the neurobiology associated with each (Hammack, Cooper, & Lexak, 2012). As previously discussed, clients who have lived with a substance-abusing family member are vulnerable to both depression and PTSD. In addition, individuals who live with a substance-abusing family member also struggle with the issue of control. They are often unable to discern where they do and do not truly have the control to affect a life circumstance (McIlveen, 2014). When someone lives with a substance-abusing family member, he or she is likely to attempt to control circumstances specifically related to the familial substance abuse. Effecting a change in the behavior of the family member struggling with an SUD is far more likely to fail than be realized, thus reinforcing a sense of helplessness. Children are particularly vulnerable to this cycle. Because children are egocentric, they believe that they are responsible for the family dysfunction and can therefore effect critical changes within the system. They will oftentimes try a multitude of strategies to shape family functioning, believing that if they can simply do the right thing or stop doing to the wrong thing, the family will change. Children are ultimately destined to fail in this endeavor. They cannot control the behavior of other family members, and their attempts to fix the family are fated to fall short. When this failure occurs over years and multiple attempts, these individuals may begin to internalize a sense of helplessness that becomes generalized (Hammack et al., 2012).

This sense of learned helplessness can present in a number of ways. These clients may assume that failure is inevitable. In fact, they may sometimes self-sabotage in order to replay what is comfortable and familiar. A client might report knowing that he or she cannot be successful in relationships. In exploring this concern, it may become clear that the client continuously chooses partners who are essentially unavailable. Or a client may report career-related or academic difficulties and feel helpless to influence his or her work or school situation. As this issue is processed, patterns in which the client creates barriers to success in these areas of life might become apparent.

Case Example for Learned Helplessness
• • •

Bud, a 44-year-old Caucasian man, has come for counseling after being laid off from his job. Bud reports that he was anticipating the lay-off and so was surprised at the intensity of his reaction to it. Bud had worked for this company for 6 years, where he was a top-level executive. As a result, he received a generous severance package that will supply a financial cushion for several months.

Bud reports a feeling of paralysis regarding the lay-off and feels certain that he will be unable to find another job. His wife has suggested that he begin to engage in activities that will help him find another job, but Bud is adamant that there is nothing he can do right now to prepare for the transition to a new job. Bud's wife is getting frustrated at his negativity and his inability to be more proactive.

Bud has been married to Joan for 8 years, and they have one child, Olivia, age 3. Bud reports that he loves his family and that this is a part of his current predicament. He feels that he is letting them down, but he feels helpless in finding any way to move forward. He is sure that he will never be able to support his family again. Bud's wife, Joan, is a successful attorney and brings in a good salary. Prior to the lay-off, the couple was extremely comfortable financially, and in fact this remains the case. Although Bud states that he knows this on a rational level, he still feels doomed to an unproductive, meaningless life.

Reflection

At this point, the counselor is likely to begin to understand the depth of Bud's sense of helplessness. In addition, it seems that this reaction to the loss of his job is not entirely rational. The counselor is likely to consider exploring the roots of Bud's sense of helplessness. Bud has been successful in the past. Therefore, his current certainty that his future is outside of his control or ability to influence is not clear.

As sessions continue, Bud begins to reveal important incidents from his childhood, beginning by sharing that the black cloud over his entire childhood was his brother's heroin addiction. Bud's brother, Adam, was 5 years older than Bud and began to experiment with drugs and alcohol at the age of 11. By the time he was 15, Adam was addicted to heroin. Having begun his addiction using pain pills, specifically OxyContin, Adam turned to heroin as his cravings and level of use increased. Heroin was both more easily accessible and less expensive.

Bud and Adam lived with their mother, their parents having divorced when Bud was 4. Bud recalls that his mother was always working and was extremely anxious regarding Adam's drug use. He recalls feeling that he needed to be good and even excel in order to avoid stressing his mother further. Bud was an extraordinarily good student and excelled in sports. He recalls believing that if he could continue to excel, he could make everything OK. And so Bud continued to work hard and excel and eventually got into a highly prestigious college.

However, during his college years and throughout his young adulthood, Bud began to struggle with his own mental health issues. He was highly anxious and depressed. Although he managed to finish school, he also got into some legal trouble and found himself aimless for a time. Bud recalls vividly his feelings of failure throughout this time. Not only did he fail to save his family (his mother, in particular), he was not even able to find a successful path for himself.

Eventually, Bud found the job with the firm he has been laid off from. Although the job was not an ideal fit for him, he was relieved to be working and earning good money. Now he feels like he has taken a giant step back into the past and has difficulty imagining how he will ever be successful again.

Implications for the Counselor

Bud is clearly feeling helpless as well as hopeless. It seems that in this case, Bud's recent lay-off has triggered a reaction that is clearly linked to his past. In fact, Bud was entirely helpless throughout his childhood. He was not able to affect his family's situation in any meaningful way. He was not ever going to be able to rescue his mother, and he was not going to have a discernible impact on his brother's drug use. However, Bud's childhood mind created a scenario in which he could control his environment. When this scenario did not become realized, Bud became anxious and depressed. Instead of exerting control where he might succeed (i.e., on his own future, his schoolwork, his search for a meaningful path), he assumed that he was helpless. The current life event of the lay-off is now triggering that same response, and Bud is consumed by a sense of doubt and helplessness. In fact, there are a number of things that Bud can do to influence his future, and he does have a significant amount of control over what he chooses to do next. However, he does not believe this to be the case.

The counselor might want to continue to explore Bud's past in the context of what is happening now. Perhaps as the patterns he has developed become clearer, Bud can begin to consider where he truly does and does not have control. At that point, the counselor may be able to assist Bud in taking some risks with exerting control in ways that might foster growth for him.

Discussion Questions

1. How do you think Bud developed learned helplessness as a coping strategy? How do you see the learned helplessness as manifesting for Bud?
2. How does Bud's childhood with familial substance abuse play a role in the development of learned helplessness as a coping strategy?
3. How would you begin to develop a treatment plan for Bud? What would you want to focus on in counseling?

Dissociation

Dissociation refers to distancing and disconnecting in the face of highly emotionally charged experiences. This process ultimately results in a restricted range of emotional response or a lack of authentic expression of feelings. From a psychological standpoint, dissociation involves the individual splitting the personality. Dissociating creates a state in which the individual is able to disconnect from parts or all of the self. Dissociation is thought to be connected to issues of trauma and prolonged exposure to a trauma-inducing environment, and individuals who live with substance abusers are vulnerable to it as a defense mechanism or as an adaptive or protective strategy. In order to protect themselves from the intensity of feelings that might be associated with living with a substance-abusing individual, a family member might begin to disconnect from the full impact of those feelings in order to effectively function (Blum, 2013; Harkness, 2001).

For any individual living with a family member struggling with an SUD, feeling the full weight of the chaos and dysfunction that exists within the family requires the genuine acknowledgment of a very difficult reality. Also, because of the ingrained denial that has likely been adopted by the family, members are not permitted to experience the true extent of their feelings or to acknowledge the reality of the situation within the family. Instead, they learn to minimize their emotional experiences associated with living with a substance-abusing family member. Engaging in this kind of numbing requires that individuals disconnect from parts of themselves. In doing this, they create a protected self that is incapable of genuine intimacy (Douglass, 2010).

Dissociation is most commonly experienced as minimizing the intensity of feelings associated with highly emotionally charged life events. For example, while recounting an episode in which the substance-abusing family member was out of control and raging, the client may have flat or no affect, expressing a limited emotional response to the incident. If this defense mechanism has been enduring, the client is likely to have generalized this type of emotional response to other situations and may react to current life events in a similar manner. Oftentimes, these individuals are unaware of what might be a more typical reaction to an emotionally laden experience. Instead, they characterize incidents that would evoke an intensity of emotion for many people as normal life events.

Case Example for Dissociation
• • •

Eleanor, a 46-year-old mother of two, has come for counseling. She reports feeling disconnected and numb. Most recently, this experience of low or no affect has begun to affect her relationship with her partner, Michelle. Eleanor reports that this relationship is extremely important to her, and yet she can feel that it is changing. Michelle has attempted to address her concerns with the distance she feels in their relationship, and Eleanor finds herself checking out and having tremendous difficulty engaging in these emotionally laden discussions. Instead, she retreats internally and winds up feeling very little. Eleanor reports knowing that she does not want to have this reaction and that she does not want to lose Michelle. However, when Michelle attempts to share her feelings or expresses anger in any way, Eleanor finds that she automatically disconnects and feels numb.

Eleanor had been married previously to a man and has two sons. She describes that in her mid 20s, she met Josh, a charismatic, attractive psychologist. She reports being astounded that he was interested in her. Although Josh openly flirted with other women, showed up late for engagements on a regular basis, and showed very little interest in her feelings and desires, she did not initially see this as a problem. She knew that Josh was damaged, but was sure that she could fix him. Over time, however, Josh's behavior became more and more unpredictable, with anger and contempt tending to dominate his mood a good deal of the time. Eleanor dealt with this by assuming more and more responsibility for the tasks of daily living. She said that she was hoping that if she could reduce the stress on Josh, maybe things could be better. However, as time went on, Josh became increasingly verbally abusive and eventually began to engage in a series of affairs. Eventually, the marriage ended.

Eleanor spent 4 years alone before she met Michelle. That was 7 years ago, and Eleanor reports that it has been a strong and stable relationship throughout that time. Recently, however,

Eleanor is noticing a shift in her relationship with Michelle. In the early years of their relationship, when Eleanor's sons were younger, they spent much of their time coparenting the boys. They did a lot together as a family and spent time chauffeuring and attending sporting events. As the boys have gotten older, Eleanor reports that it has been nice to have time to do more adult things with Michelle. They have traveled and have begun finding activities to enjoy together. However, recently, Eleanor notices that she and Michelle are gravitating toward different interests and that they are fighting more than they have in the past. Eleanor finds that she is responding to this change by shutting down and pulling away. She notices that the more she pulls away, the angrier Michelle seems to get. However, she feels paralyzed and unable to reconnect once Michelle gets angry. They both agree that they want to reconnect and work on their relationship. However, Eleanor does not know how to do this.

Reflection

Up to this point in the counseling process, the counselor might be imagining that Eleanor is reflexively invoking a defense mechanism that she has used in the past. Although it remains unclear what the issue is between her and Michelle that is distancing them, it is clear that Eleanor is responding in a manner that may not invite healing. The counselor may wish to more fully explore the source of the changes in the relationship and then assist Eleanor in exploring her response to her distress.

As Eleanor begins to share more, she describes her childhood as fairly chaotic and stressful. Her mother had an AUD, and her father was verbally abusive in ways that left her feeling worthless and unsure of herself. Her earliest memories include ongoing fighting between her parents. Eleanor remembers dreading the return of her father from work because she knew that the evening would be explosive and scary. She reports that, as things at home got worse, she simply tried harder to be "good." When this did not work, Eleanor began to retreat. As an only child, Eleanor did not have siblings to retreat with. Instead, she describes spending a tremendous amount of time alone in her room with her headphones on so that she did not have to hear the ongoing fighting between her parents.

When Eleanor was an adolescent, she recalls her mother's drinking getting worse and her father becoming more and more abusive. In fact, Eleanor describes scenes in which her father would scream at her and she would simply stand there until he was done and then walk away. She claims that she could almost feel the wall come up as he began his rants. Eleanor would simply endure the screaming and then leave, never demonstrating any emotional reaction. When the counselor asks about her mother, Eleanor states that she does not recall her mother being available during those times. She knew she was alone and had to figure out how to endure the tirades independently.

Although the current situation in which Michelle has expressed anger toward Eleanor might feel similar to what she experienced as an adolescent, Eleanor has not made this connection. She reports that she is utterly confused at her reaction to Michelle's anger. She knows that she should listen and respond and attempt to engage in the difficult conversations, but she feels that her automatic response of disconnecting is intractable. However, as the counselor and Eleanor continue to explore her past responses to anger, Eleanor begins to see the connection to her present-day behavior. As counseling continues and Eleanor becomes increasingly aware of her use of dissociation as an automatic defense mechanism, she begins to practice staying present and engaging in the difficult discussions. As a result, she and Michelle are able to begin the process of uncovering the sources of the changes in their relationship.

Implications for the Counselor

In this case, Eleanor learned to use dissociation as a survival tool. In the face of her father's unrelenting rage, Eleanor learned to shut down, detach, and become numb. Although this was an appropriate and possibly even advantageous defensive strategy when she was an adolescent dealing with her father, it was not working in her adult life. In this case, the counselor effectively helped Eleanor explore the origins of her using shutting down as a coping strategy: her experiences with her father. Once this connection was solidified for Eleanor, she was able to experiment with not shutting down in her interactions with Michelle.

When a client uses defense mechanisms or coping strategies that are no longer useful—and perhaps are even deleterious—he or she must become aware of the automatic responses that have taken hold. In Eleanor's case, this response involved shutting down immediately, leaving the other person (i.e., Michelle) alone with the issue. When individuals disconnect emotionally in relationships, there is no longer an avenue open to explore the issue being raised. This situation usually results in the initiators getting angry, as they generally feel that they are attempting to address a concern and are not being heard or even acknowledged. This is precisely what was happening with Michelle and Eleanor. The only means of combating this pattern is by paying attention, acknowledging when the automatic response emerges, and challenging that response in an effort to find a way to stay connected and engaged. This process will generally become the work to be done in the counseling process.

Discussion Questions

1. How do you think Eleanor developed dissociation as a coping strategy?
2. How did Eleanor's mother's alcoholism play a role in Eleanor's acquisition of dissociation as a defense mechanism?
3. How would you begin to develop a treatment plan for Eleanor? What would you want to focus on in counseling?

Hypervigilance

Vigilance is defined as the act of being keenly watchful in order to detect danger (Vigilance, n.d.). The state of hypervigilance includes increased sensory activity and an exaggerated intensity of feelings and behaviors required to detect threats (Tull, 2008). A hypervigilant individual is likely to continuously scan the environment for possible threats. From a psychological perspective, this hypervigilance is specifically targeted at identifying possible emotional threats. In other words, a hypervigilant individual is virtually always on the lookout for any interaction that might elicit an uncomfortable psychological state. This constant state of sensory excitation is accompanied by increased anxiety; in fact, the physiological response to both is identical. That is, the body does not distinguish between hypervigilance and anxiety; therefore, the individual is likely to eventually reach a physiological state of exhaustion. From a psychological standpoint, the impact of hypervigilance includes an inability to be present, as the present moment is often lost to the constant scanning of the environment. For individuals who are hypervigilant, this heightened sensory state is always present, even in the face of neutral stimuli (Kimble et al., 2014). A heightened state of sensory excitation is especially problematic for developing children. Research suggests that ongoing high levels of stress can affect the architecture of the brain. To be specific, circuitry development is vulnerable to neglect during the first year of life (Vela, 2014). Again, children being raised by a primary caregiver with an SUD are at an increased risk of being neglected, and the impact of this neglect extends to the development of brain circuitry during the earliest years of life.

Individuals who live with a substance-abusing family member are more likely to be hypervigilant than those who do not (Hussong et al., 2008; Hussong & Chassin, 2004). It is presumed that the relationship between familial substance abuse and increased levels of hypervigilance is the result of interactional patterns that are established while the individual is living with the substance-abusing family member. As discussed previously, families that include a member with an SUD are likely to be unpredictable and chaotic. This environment leads other family members to be on high alert to possible incidents associated with the substance abuser's behavior. This response is based in reality. In other words, the substance abuser's behavior and mood do, in fact, affect the family in a very direct and real way. Hypervigilance, as a response to this reality, makes perfect sense. However, a state of constant arousal, and the accompanying fear that danger is imminent, does not necessarily serve the individual well in other settings. Nevertheless, for individuals who have lived with substance abusers, hypervigilance has often become habitual and automatic and is generalized to virtually every situation in their life. This automatic response can greatly interfere with an individual's present-day overall psychological well-being. For example, hypervigilance precludes the ability to attend to present-moment activities and feelings. In addition, a constant state of hypervigilance does not allow for emotional comfort or contentedness. Over the long term, hypervigilance is also likely to interfere with physical well-being. For the chronically hypervigilant individual, the physiological stress reaction is likely to be triggered on a frequent basis. The physiological response to stress involves the activation of systems within the body intended to protect humans from occasional events associated with real danger. This activated state of heightened sensory ability is not meant to become the normal or typical physiological state for human beings (Kimble et al., 2014).

Case Example for Hypervigilance
• • •

Antonio, a 26-year-old Italian American man, has come for counseling to address his anxiety. Antonio is in the second semester of study in a counselor education program and reports that "getting therapy" is highly recommended within the program. He states that in his studies he has had several opportunities to engage in self-reflection and is more aware of his inability to relax or feel a sense of calm.

Antonio reports that he has been in a relationship with Tom for the past 6 months and describes this relationship as significant, as it is the first "real relationship" he has been in since he came out as gay 2 years ago. He describes his relationship as "fine" but reports that it is difficult for him to maintain a sense of calm even when he and Tom are together. He says that they met one evening in a local club and proceeded to date for a month or two before deciding to move in together. They have been living together for about four months, during which time Antonio has noticed that Tom has a tendency to drink quite a bit.

As Antonio begins to share the events and circumstances of his childhood, he reveals that he grew up in a typical Italian family.

Both of his parent emigrated from Italy as young adults, shortly after getting married. Antonio's uncle had moved to the United States earlier and had started a successful construction business. Antonio's father worked in the family business. His mother stayed home and cared for him and his younger brother and sister.

Antonio goes on to share that his father was a "raging alcoholic." His childhood memories revolve around his fear of his father coming home at the end of the day. He states that he never knew which father he was going to get, as his father's moods were erratic and unpredictable. In the event that he had had a bad day, Antonio's father was likely to come home drunk and enraged. He remembers his mother being fearful, and Antonio worked hard to help her feel safe. But this effort did not prevent his father from becoming enraged at almost anything. Although Antonio states that there was not a lot of physical violence, such abuse was not entirely absent. Antonio was generally the target of the physical abuse, and he shares that he was glad that was the case, as he wanted to protect his mother and his younger siblings.

Reflection

In working with Antonio, the counselor might begin to piece together a hypothesis regarding his inability to relax and feel comfortable. Antonio lived through a number of developmental stages in an environment that was extremely unpredictable and often frightening. Never being able to predict what his evenings might involve has likely left Antonio with a heightened degree of attentiveness to his surroundings. Chronic hypervigilance would be a natural response to such an experience. Perhaps Antonio has unwittingly carried this hypervigilance into his adult life. In addition, Antonio is now partnered and living with Tom, whom he has described as a heavy drinker. Perhaps Tom's drinking behavior, even if it is not coupled with rage-filled outbursts, reinforces Antonio's hypervigilance.

As Antonio continues his story, he begins to share his ongoing and pervasive feelings of fear. He states that he almost never feels safe and finds that when he enters a new situation, his first inclination is to assess the threat risk. For example, he will go to a party with Tom and while other guests appear to be mingling and socializing, he finds himself sizing people up and wondering if they will like him or if any of them might threaten his relationship with Tom. When someone at the party engages Antonio in a conversation, he immediately wonders what they really think of him.

As Antonio begins to talk more about his relationship with Tom, he describes the same level of "being on guard" on a consistent basis. He finds himself monitoring Tom's drinking; however, he has been unable to talk with Tom directly about his feelings regarding drinking. As the counselor and Antonio continue to explore his concerns regarding Tom's drinking behavior, Antonio reports that Tom generally has either a glass of wine or a beer every night, sometimes two on weekend nights. Although Antonio is cognitively aware that this is not indicative of a substance abuse problem, he is worried that Tom's drinking will increase. When the counselor and Antonio begin to explore Tom's behavior, Antonio reports that Tom rarely gets angry, and that they are generally able to resolve disagreements. Still, Antonio is afraid to speak directly with Tom about his feelings surrounding the whole issue of drinking.

Implications for the Counselor

Treatment for Antonio will include the same kind of rapport building and trust building previously noted as imperative to working with any client who has lived with an individual with an SUD. Because trust has likely been broken for this population of clients, it is likely that this part of the therapeutic process may take longer and require higher levels of empathy. Once a relationship has been firmly established, helping Antonio look at his hypervigilance makes sense. Initially, the counselor might try to further explore Antonio's fears regarding Tom's drinking, as these do not appear to be based in reality.

The counselor might also want to explore whether or not there are any instances in which Antonio feels relaxed or able to let his guard down. In this way, the counselor can assess whether the hypervigilance that Antonio experiences is in fact generalized to virtually all settings or if there are times of genuine relaxation and comfort in his life. If the latter is the case, perhaps the counselor and Antonio can explore what is different about the relaxing situations.

In the event that the hypervigilance experienced by Antonio is persistent and ever-present, perhaps the counselor can begin to explore with Antonio whether the hypervigilance he currently experiences is rooted in present-day reality and if he might be safer than he imagines in his current life. As with many individuals' responses to living with a family member with an SUD, Antonio may be responding to internally embedded signals and reactions that are not in fact necessary and helpful in his current life. This exploration can be done by continuing to use relationship-building skills and techniques in conjunction with cognitive approaches that might assist Antonio in understanding his current-day reality and the extent to which he might be using hypervigilance at times when it is not truly necessary.

Discussion Questions

1. How would you explain Antonio's apparent hypervigilance?
2. How might you consider working with Antonio on the issue of hypervigilance if he appeared completely unaware of this as an issue?

3. How might you work with Antonio to assess his present-day life to determine the reality of emotional or psychological threat?

Low Self-Esteem

According to Rosenberg (1965), author of the Rosenberg Self-Esteem Scale, *self-esteem* is defined as an individual's evaluation of his or her worth. Described as one facet of an individual's overall self-concept, self-esteem refers specifically to the level of regard one has for oneself or the level of value one places on one's well-being. Two of the components of self-esteem include feeling a sense of accomplishment in the world and seeing oneself on an equal plane with others in terms of worthiness. Level of self-esteem is regarded as important to one's overall sense of psychological well-being. In fact, it has been cited as essential to overall mental health, and low levels of it are a key indicator of psychological distress (Macaskill & Denovan, 2014).

Although research suggests that many factors influence the development of self-esteem, the role of early attachment in the development of a consistent sense of worth is a theme evident throughout the literature (Lecompte, Moss, Cyr, & Pascuzzo, 2014; Mikulincer, Shaver, Bar-On, & Sahdra, 2014; Otway & Carnelley, 2013). In addition, self-esteem has been linked to the perceived quality of important relationships within our lives (Erol & Orth, 2014; Tackett, Nelson, & Busby, 2013). The extent to which we value ourselves is directly related to how we experience ourselves in the primary relationships in our lives. This connection is extremely important. Throughout life, individuals are likely to make critical decisions (e.g., who to become intimately involved with) on the basis of, at least in part, their level of self-esteem (Macaskill & Denovan, 2014). This judgment of self-worth has the potential to inform many aspects of life and is an essential component to psychological health—something that is true for all client populations. However, in the case of clients who have a family member with an SUD, there is a high likelihood of disruptions in primary relationships, which results in low self-esteem. In fact, low self-esteem should be considered a potential issue for any client who has lived with a substance-abusing individual (Love Longman, 2014).

In virtually every study comparing levels of self-esteem between COAs and children of nonalcoholics, those who experience parental substance use and abuse showed lower levels of self-esteem (Park & Schepp, 2014). A high level of chaos within the family has also been linked to low self-esteem for children in such families (Love Longman, 2014; Rangarajan, 2008), and as established previously, chaos is in fact a hallmark of families with a substance-abusing member. Thus, clients with a history of familial SUD are at an increased risk of struggling with issues related to self-esteem and self-worth.

Case Example for Low Self-Esteem
• • •

Matt is a junior at a rural high school. He works hard and is a gifted artist, a skill that has gotten him a great deal of attention throughout his years within the public school system. In addition, Matt gets good grades and plays football, his father's favorite sport. When Matt's school counselor calls him in for a post-high school planning session, the counselor immediately notices Matt's flat affect. When asked about his future plans, Matt responds casually that he will do whatever his father wants him to do. When the counselor brings up Matt's exceptional art skills, especially in painting, Matt dismisses the idea of pursuing art, saying that his family wouldn't like that. The counselor is aware of Matt's discomfort in talking openly about his future and asks him if he would consider coming in a few more times to talk. After some hesitation, Matt agrees to see the school counselor a few times to talk about interests and possibilities for his future.

In their first session, Matt explains that his primary concern in life is keeping his father happy and proud. In fact, he is unwilling to consider options for his future that he does not believe would please his father. As the counselor attempts to probe more deeply, he is dismayed to discover that Matt seems to be unable to describe himself or his interests. The counselor decides to direct the conversation to Matt's family and to his father in particular. As they begin to explore this part of his life, Matt reveals that his father drinks often. However, when the counselor attempts to probe this issue, Matt becomes defensive and claims that "It's not a big deal; he's a lawyer, so he has a very stressful job."

Reflection

In working with Matt, the counselor is likely to notice Matt's inability to value his own desires. In fact, Matt is unable to consider making decisions regarding his life that he is not certain will please his father. In addition, the counselor is likely to be struck by the comment Matt made regarding his father's drinking, as well as his reluctance to discuss this issue. This reluctance may indicate denial, or it may indicate that this is a topic that is off limits. In either case, the counselor might attempt to explore this issue further.

As the year progresses, the counselor continues to meet with Matt on a regular basis. After establishing a rapport with Matt and working on building trust, the counselor begins to probe for issues regarding Matt's sense of self. However, this process proves difficult as Matt continues to assert that his primary goal is to please his father. In fact, Matt's sense of worth is inextricably tied to the extent to which he feels he would please his father. In exploring his father's drinking, Matt reveals that on some level, he feels responsible for that. He is convinced that if he could figure out the precise recipe for pleasing his father, he would be able to control his father's drinking. However, no matter how hard Matt tries, he has been unable to "fix" his father. He views this as his failure and repeatedly reports feeling worthless.

As Matt became more trusting of the counselor and more comfortable discussing his life at home, he begins to report specific episodes in which his father's drinking has been problematic. He describes one evening when he could hear his parents fighting and then heard his mother crying. He decided to see if he could intervene so he asked his father to look over his homework. However, his father was furious with the interruption and screamed at Matt to get back to his room where he belonged.

Implications for the Counselor

In this case, the school counselor is likely to focus on Matt's sense of worthlessness and low self-esteem. Matt has linked his sense of self-worth to his father's approval and happiness. He feels responsible for his father's sense of well-being and believes that he can ultimately control his father's drinking.

The counselor is likely to use several approaches in working with Matt. Initially, the counselor may include a psychoeducational component within the counseling. To be specific, this component could include some education related to addiction and substance abuse and how that looks in families. This process may lead to a more in-depth exploration of Matt's feelings of control over his father's happiness and behavior. At the same time, the counselor will want to work on establishing an increasingly deeper level of trust in his or her relationship with Matt. The issues related to Matt's low self-esteem are tied to a sense of secrecy and perhaps deep shame at being unable to "fix" his father.

Finally, the counselor will want to work on Matt's sense of worthlessness using a variety of techniques and theoretical perspectives. From a cognitive framework, the counselor may wish to appeal to the logic of Matt's ability to change his father. In addition, using this theoretical perspective, the counselor may want to attempt to work with Matt on identifying what he in fact can control and thus work toward exploring more of his own interests and talents.

Discussion Questions

1. How do you see Matt's inability to consider his future apart from his father's expectations and well-being as related to his level of self-esteem?
2. How do you see Matt's level of self-esteem as it might relate to his future if left unaddressed?
3. How is Matt's sense of worthlessness related to his father's issues with alcohol? Is it important to help Matt see this connection?

Chapter 8

Relational Consequences of Living With a Person With an SUD

There are other potential consequences of living with a family member struggling with an SUD. Oftentimes, family members of substance abusers struggle in their relationships. In fact, there are potential relational consequences that have been shown to exist for this population of clients (see Table 7). Those potential relational consequences are the focus of this chapter.

Inability for Healthy Bonding

It is widely assumed that healthy attachment in very early childhood is a prerequisite for a lifelong ability to engage in relationships that are healthy and growth promoting. In fact, healthy attachment security has been linked to an increase in overall life satisfaction, whereas a lack of attachment security has been linked to an increased risk for both depression and loneliness (Pielage, Luteijn, & Arrindell, 2005). In addition, early bonding memories have been linked to attachment styles in adulthood. Individuals who recall securely bonding in their earliest relationships report more secure attachment styles in adulthood. On the other hand, when individuals maintain that early attachment needs were not adequately met, the resulting automatic bonding style tends to be fearful (Ambruster, 2008).

Table 7
Relational Consequences of Living With an Individual Struggling With an SUD

Consequence	Description
Inability for healthy bonding	Inability to create healthy adult relationships that are balanced
Boundary issues	Inability to maintain healthy emotional boundaries in relationships
Lack of assertiveness	Inability to express one's thoughts, desires, beliefs, or feelings in a healthy but firm manner
Attraction to narcissism	Attracted to individuals with a narcissistic personality disorder; learning to attend almost exclusively to the needs of others
Inability to maintain an authentic self	Feel the need to hide parts of the self; excessive worry over about how they will be perceived or received

Note. SUD = substance use disorder.

As discussed earlier, in families where a member is struggling with an SUD, early attachment can be negatively affected. To be specific, for children living in homes where one or both parents is abusing substances, the kind of early attachment necessary to develop healthy ways of relating in the world may be compromised. In turn, the ability to create and maintain healthy adult relationships is likely to be compromised. In fact, COAs have been shown to have lower levels of relationship satisfaction than their non-COA peers (Kelley et al., 2010). This lower level of relationship satisfaction may take the form of a perceived inability to connect on an emotional level with others, or, at the other extreme, relationships may be characterized as enmeshed or fused, as oftentimes children of parents with SUD have difficulty with healthy bonding. Healthy bonding involves the ability to connect emotionally with another adult, which requires the development of trust, healthy boundaries, and ways of relating that are respectful and meaningful. Adults theoretically achieve this status as a result of healthy development throughout childhood and adolescence. However, adults raised by parents with an SUD tend toward adult relationships characterized by insecure, fearful, or avoidant attachment patterns, making healthy bonding in adulthood virtually impossible (Raffaela, 2013).

Case Study of Inability for Healthy Bonding
• • •
Walter, a 58-year-old African American man, has come for counseling. He reports that a coworker he is friendly with recommended that it might be a good idea for him to talk with someone. Walter had been talking to his friend about his history

with failed relationships and the fact that his current relationship seems to be following the same predictable pattern. Walter reports that he has been dating Wendy for about 2 years. They met online, and Walter states that they have a tremendous amount in common. In addition, he describes the relationship as likely the healthiest he has ever had. He claims that he and Wendy are able to communicate well, are extremely respectful of each other, and share many interests. Despite this, Walter feels certain that he will sabotage this relationship, as this is his pattern. He has decided to come for counseling because he wants to be in a healthy intimate relationship and is aware that he has been repeatedly unable to achieve this throughout his entire adulthood.

Walter begins to share that, although he knows that his current relationship with Wendy is the best he has ever had, he feels anxious and extremely ambivalent. He reports feeling ongoing doubt. When asked to elaborate on these thoughts, Walter describes picking out small details that might indicate that he should not be in this relationship. For example, sometimes Wendy is quiet in social situations. Walter, on the other hand, is outgoing, and he worries that maybe he should not be with someone who is quieter and more reserved. And while he is passionate about music, Wendy's passions include movies and reading. Walter states that he knows that the important things are very solid in this relationship, but he is unable to commit or even relax and enjoy his time with Wendy.

Reflection

Walter's ambivalence is confusing at this point. The counselor might be wondering why Walter is experiencing such high levels of discomfort associated with this relationship. He describes a respectful, fulfilling relationship that he is unable to fully embrace. At this point, the counselor might want to explore what has happened in Walter's life that evokes this kind of response to intimacy.

As the counseling continues, the counselor begins to explore Walter's relationship history. Walter admits that intimacy has always been a huge issue for him. He has never been married and describes a long series of relationships that eventually end. Walter is very aware that he is the cause of most of these endings and admits that when he reaches the point he is currently at with Wendy, he usually begins to push the other person away. He becomes distant and critical about small things that are not truly important. In addition, the thoughts regarding why he should not be in the current relationship increase.

As Walter begins to describe his childhood, he reports being the only child of a single mother. In fact, his mother had an affair with a married man and got pregnant. He describes his childhood as highly stressful. Walter's mother worked in a local school cafeteria, and financial stresses were always evident. In addition, Walter describes his mother as very needy and extremely attached to him. Walter can recall his discomfort with the level of closeness his mother seemed to require. In addition, Walter's mother was depressed and anxious, and she abused Valium for as long as he can remember. He remembers her going away for treatment several times, only to ultimately return to using.

Implications for the Counselor

In the case of Walter, the counselor sees a client who has been unable to achieve a healthy adult bond in the context of an intimate relationship. As Walter shares his childhood experiences, and particularly his relationship with his mother, the counselor learns that this relationship was highly stressful for Walter. Although Walter is obviously unable to recall the first year of his life, the counselor might suspect that the attachment between him and his mother was anxious. This anxious attachment, in conjunction with the fact that his mother struggled with an SUD throughout his childhood, may have set the stage for Walter's difficulties with intimacy in adulthood.

Again, the establishment of a therapeutic alliance with Walter will likely be the initial goal in working with him. The counselor is then likely to help Walter explore the connections between his relationship with his mother and his experiences with adult relationships. In Walter's description of the internal process that takes place for him upon entering a potentially intimate relationship, he reports thoughts that he experiences as automatic. In this case, the counselor might consider the use of cognitive therapy as a means of helping Walter challenge these automatic thoughts. Perhaps a strategy for dealing with these thoughts can be mutually explored. In this way, Walter might be able to consider the source of the reactions that prohibit intimacy.

Discussion Questions

1. Do you think that Walter's inability for healthy bonding is related to earlier experiences?
2. How do you see Walter's inability for healthy bonding as related to growing up in a family with a substance-abusing member?
3. Is it important for Walter to make the connection between his earlier experiences and his current-day struggles? How would you facilitate this understanding?

Boundary Issues

Boundaries exist in all families and are described as the invisible lines that separate the various subsystems within a family (e.g., spouses, parents, children, individuals; Piercy & Sprenkle, 1988). Boundaries are considered essential to healthy relationships, as they serve the important function of helping to preserve the independence of the subsystem while maintaining interdependence with other family subsystems (Marrett, Sprenkle, & Lewis, 1992). Boundaries in families are important in maintaining the balance of distance and closeness within relationships and help to regulate the flow of communication. This fact is true both inside and outside of the family, although people's introduction to boundaries and how they operate occurs very early in life within the family system.

According to family systems theory (Gladding, 2014), boundaries can exist in three different ways: healthy, diffuse, and rigid. Healthy boundaries are characterized by appropriate rules and roles while remaining flexible enough to allow for change. Diffuse boundaries are characterized by enmeshed relationships that prevent autonomy and differentiation, as there is an overflow of information passed between the subsystems. On the other hand, rigid boundaries are characterized by disengaged relationships where autonomy and independence occur at the expense of almost all connection and very little information is allowed to pass through (Ramisch, McVicker, & Sahin, 2009).

As discussed earlier, in families with a member who abuses drugs or alcohol, the SUD becomes the organizing mechanism for that family's homeostasis. As a result, these families organize themselves around denial, shame, and control. When these issues constitute the organizational structure of a family, poor boundaries tend to emerge. According to Salvador Minuchin (2006), dysfunctional families have difficulty with emotional bonding and with individual autonomy. Thus, families with a substance-abusing member tend to fluctuate between rigid and diffuse boundaries. Both of these extremes affect the family's ability to function effectively as a unit. In addition, rigid or diffuse boundaries within a family do not facilitate optimal development for the individual family members. Rigid boundaries promote development in the absence of connection, encouraging distance in primary relationships. On the other hand, diffuse boundaries occur in an environment where development takes place in the context of enmeshed close relationships, creating the expectation that all relationships are characterized by dependency and a lack of autonomous functioning (Minuchin, 1974). In either case, the developing individual is learning and internalizing the concept of boundaries and how they are maintained in close relationships.

Case Example for Boundary Issues
• • •

Maria is a 12-year-old seventh grader who has been referred to her school counselor by one of her teachers, who observed unusual behavior. Once a hard-working, straight-A student, Maria has recently stopped completing her assignments and is receiving failing grades. In addition, her appearance has changed. Whereas

Maria historically dressed in the manner of her middle school peers, she has recently come to school disheveled. In addition, she appears tired and has been dozing off in class.

Maria is the oldest child in a middle-class Puerto Rican American family. She has two younger siblings: Henry, age 9, and Carmela, age 7. Both Henry and Carmela attend the local elementary school. Maria's father currently holds two jobs, and her mother works full time as well. As a result, Maria has always had responsibilities at home that include helping out with her younger sister and brother and completing a variety of chores around the house.

In her first session with the school counselor, Maria discloses that her mother and father have been arguing a lot for the past few weeks, keeping her up at night. She claims that there has always been some tension in the house, but that things seem to be worse lately. Maria shares that her mother cries more frequently, and her father is more distant and absent than ever.

As the counselor probes further, Maria states that her father does seem to drink a lot of beer. There are many evenings when Maria's father comes home from work and goes straight to the basement. In fact, Maria reports that she and her siblings sometimes go several nights without seeing him. However, recently, it is becoming more common for Maria's father to stay out all night. When he does come home, he is visibly intoxicated and either goes straight down to the basement or goes to bed.

Maria knows that this behavior is the cause of her mother's recent sadness, as she confides in Maria regarding her loneliness and unhappiness in her marriage, often keeping Maria up well into the night. Maria is conflicted in terms of how she feels about these conversations. She states that it is "weird and uncomfortable" to hear these things from her mother. However, she also feels special and is glad that she can be there for her mother and play this important role.

When the counselor shifts the conversation to Maria's academic functioning, Maria admits to not spending much time recently focusing on her studies. Instead, she has been taking care of her two younger siblings: getting them organized for the upcoming school day, making their lunches for school, and helping them with homework.

Reflection

As the counselor continues to work with Maria, it becomes evident that her father is likely struggling with an SUD. As a result, her family is experiencing dysfunction. To be specific, the boundary between Maria and her mother is extremely diffuse. In fact, Maria has taken on a parentified role in the family that includes caring for herself and her younger siblings and acting as an emotional support for her mother. There is an inappropriate flow of communication between Maria and her mother, which could affect the development of Maria's identity and level of differentiation.

As Maria continues to share, she describes having a close relationship with her mother, but it becomes clear that she does not like it when her mother talks about her father. Even though Maria does not spend as much time with her dad as she would like, she does not think he is a bad father, and she is uncomfortable colluding with her mother about him. She wishes things were different and that she could have a normal life. She wants to get back to attending to her academics and spending more time with her friends. However, she feels very strongly that her mother needs her right now and that she cannot abandon her.

Implications for the Counselor

In this case, the school counselor will likely want to follow up with Maria and perhaps even schedule a weekly meeting with her while they work to help Maria balance her responsibilities and ensure that her needs are being met. Although the counselor has a responsibility to facilitate Maria's academic focus and success, this is a case where the academic aspect of Maria's life is inextricably woven into the emotional struggles that she (and her family) are currently experiencing. It is Maria's relationships with her family that are directly affecting her ability to succeed in school.

A primary and immediate issue for Maria is her relationship with her mother. This relationship has become highly enmeshed, and the roles have become confused. In its current iteration, Maria is acting as the parent and, in fact, is also serving as a friend to her mother as she copes with difficulties within her marriage. The substance abuse in the family has likely affected the system's structure in ways that have changed boundaries. It will be very important for Maria to become disentangled from her current relationships and roles within her family so that she might be freed up to focus on the more typical developmental tasks associated with a 12-year-old.

Because the school counselor is limited in terms of time and scope, he or she may want to collaborate with an outside agency. In fact, the counselor may wish to meet with the mother to discuss the concerns regarding Maria and assess the family's openness to family therapy. In this way, the school counselor can continue to work with Maria and collaborate with a therapist who can assist in the treatment of the family issues and dysfunction.

Discussion Questions

1. How are issues with boundaries manifested in the case of Maria?
2. How do you think these issues relate to Maria's father's drinking?
3. What would be your goals as a school counselor working with Maria?

Lack of Assertiveness

Assertiveness is described as the ability to directly express your emotions and needs. As opposed to aggression, assertiveness involves strongly stating needs, feelings, or wishes in a manner that is neither hostile nor hurtful. It includes the use of simple, albeit strong, statements to convey a stance in an unambiguous manner. Aggressiveness, on the other hand, involves the use of coercion, manipulation, intimidation, or any other means of conveying a stance that violates the rights, safety, or dignity of another person. It is healthy and growth producing to be assertive (Turner & Langhinrichsen-Rohling, 2011). It is not healthy to be aggressive (Kunimatsu, & Marsee, 2012). It is also unhealthy to refrain from assertive behavior by avoiding the expression of your own needs, feelings, or desires. Stating one's needs in an important relationship in either a hostile manner or a withholding manner prohibits open communication within the relationship.

As with many of the other characteristics discussed so far, it is common for individuals who live with substance abusers to struggle with the concept and the act of appropriate assertiveness (Mares, van der Vorst, Engels, & Lichtwarck-Aschoff, 2011). Many individuals who live with family members struggling with an SUD have not been taught that assertiveness is necessary and valuable. Instead, these individuals often wind up at the extremes: They are likely either to become aggressive in response to situations involving conflict or unmet needs or expectations or to express no needs in response to such events. Neither of these extremes will facilitate healthy communication or lead to an optimal resolution of the issue at hand. In relationships where this type of interaction becomes a pattern, the honest sharing of what is most important to each individual is thwarted.

An individual's ability to communicate assertively is often dependent upon how the family has negotiated communication and conflict resolution within the unit. In addition, the role that an individual plays within the system will affect that individual's ability to assert himself or herself. For example, in a family that uses a highly emotional and volatile means of communicating around the needs of the individuals, the members learn to incorporate this type of communication into relationships outside of the family. Likewise, when the family extends its use of denial to include a lack of recognition of individuals' needs and feelings, members are likely to learn that expression of these things is not appropriate. These misconceptions are often generalized to other relationships, and the individual is likely to have difficulty being appropriately assertive in a variety of settings. In addition, the role that an individual plays within the family is likely to influence the extent to which he or she is able to assertively express his or her needs and feelings. The hero and the lost child may have difficulty being assertive, as they have survived by having limited needs within their family. On the other hand, the scapegoat and the mascot may express needs more aggressively or inappropriately, as they have survived within the family by drawing attention to themselves, sometimes at the expense of other members' needs.

Case Example for Lack of Assertiveness

Sandy, a 27-year-old Caucasian female, has come for counseling to address her anxiety. Sandy states that her anxiety is related to an impending move that she and her husband have decided to make to Ecuador. Sandy feels ambivalent regarding the move, and these feelings have become increasingly troublesome.

Sandy has been married to Barry for less than a year. They dated for 10 years prior to getting married, during which time they both worked toward establishing their careers. After exploring several options, Barry decided on teaching Spanish and recently completed a graduate program in teaching. Upon graduating, Barry attempted to find a job near their home. However, jobs were scarce, and Barry finally decided to expand his search. Through networking, he was eventually offered the opportunity to teach for 2 years in Ecuador.

During this same time, Sandy has worked on her career as a musician. After a number of years of floundering, she finally landed a spot as lead singer and guitarist for a local band. Sandy describes this job as a perfect fit and the job she had always dreamed of having. Her band has recently gained national recognition, and Sandy's career is well established.

Despite her career success, Sandy has decided to put her musical aspirations on hold to go to Ecuador with Barry for 2 years. Although Sandy was initially interested in staying in the United States and maintaining a long-distance relationship throughout the next 2 years, Barry convinced her that this was not a good idea. From Barry's point of view, it is very important for the two of them to live together, especially so early in their marriage. Sandy found herself easily persuaded and so thought that this was a sign that Barry was right. However, as the move draws closer, Sandy finds herself anxious about putting her career dreams on hold. She is not comfortable sharing these feelings with Barry, as she has already made a commitment to move with him. In addition, Sandy describes that the ambivalence keeps her frozen, as she is certain that she will be unable to assert her needs and desires once she engages with Barry.

Within the first few therapy sessions, Sandy begins to reveal details regarding her childhood. Sandy was born in London as the older of two children: her brother, Ian, is 3 years younger than Sandy. Sandy's mother was 20 years old when she had

Sandy, and she gave up her career as a television actress in order to work as a stay-at-home mother. Sandy's father was 20 years older than her mother and worked as a movie producer. Sandy's earliest memories include a string of parties and entertaining at their large and luxurious home in London. However, when Sandy was 10, her parents' marriage ended, and she, Ian, and her mother moved back to her mother's childhood home to live with Sandy's grandparents. Sandy's recollection of this time includes her grandfather's stern and demanding demeanor. Sandy states that she learned simply to do as she was told. Her mother was an active alcoholic during this time and worked as a bartender. She was often out all night. This behavior infuriated Sandy's grandfather, and so Sandy worked exceptionally hard trying to "make up" for her mother's transgressions. The good news, according to Sandy, is that when she was 18 years old, her mother went into a rehabilitation facility and has been sober since.

Reflection

Hearing Sandy's story allows the counselor to put Sandy's lack of assertiveness into context. Throughout her entire childhood, Sandy existed in environments where she was unable to express her needs and feelings. In fact, she felt forced to focus exclusively on the needs and desires of her family members. It appears that Sandy's survival became tied to her ability to relinquish her needs and attend to those of her family. Assertively stating her own needs and feelings would certainly be unfamiliar to Sandy and may in fact induce fear. This situation may explain her ambivalence and Barry's ability to quickly "change her mind."

As counseling with Sandy progresses, the counselor begins to encourage Sandy to explore her true desires. As Sandy slowly gains trust in the counselor and in the therapeutic process, she begins to access her genuine feelings. She is eventually able to assert—at least within the counseling relationship—her desire to stay behind and continue to pursue her career.

Implications for the Counselor

In this case, the counselor is working with a client who has likely never been assertive. Sandy may, in fact, have difficulty even understanding what this concept means. She will find it uncomfortable to acknowledge her true feelings and desires to herself and may very well resist asserting them outside of the counseling relationship, as she has likely learned that asserting herself will surely lead to a catastrophic outcome. The counselor will need to work toward establishing a trusting therapeutic relationship with Sandy in order to begin to influence what may be faulty beliefs regarding speaking up for herself. Once Sandy trusts the counselor, perhaps a more directive approach, encouraging Sandy to gradually "practice" assertiveness, can be used to encourage growth in this area.

Discussion Questions

1. How do you conceptualize Sandy's ambivalence?
2. In what ways might it be related to her childhood experiences?
3. Do you agree that an inability to assert her needs and feelings is at the root of Sandy's current anxiety?
4. How might you begin to explore these issues with Sandy?

Attraction to Narcissism

As discussed previously, it is not unusual for family members of substance abusers to develop codependent relationships (Dear et al., 2004; Douglass, 2010). These codependent relationships occur primarily as the result of the family member learning to attend almost exclusively to the needs of others, thus providing a role and purpose for that individual within the family. As a result, this individual is likely to internalize this pattern and unconsciously seek out relationships in which he or she can continue to fulfill that role. In particular, in families with an individual who has an SUD, the enabler and the hero frequently take on the role of caretaker. In this case, the individual's identity within the family becomes based on his or her ability to meet the needs of others, often at the expense of attending to his or her own needs.

As discussed previously, for an individual with a narcissistic personality disorder, identity is dependent upon reference to others for self-definition and self-esteem regulation (*DSM-5*; APA, 2013). In other words, people with narcissistic personality disorder rely on others to validate their identity. Their level of self-esteem is regulated by the extent to which others perceive them as worthy, and it generally involves the expectation of an exaggerated appraisal of their value in order to maintain a level of self-esteem that is acceptable to them. On a related note, emotional regulation for a person with narcissistic personality disorder is dependent on fluctuations in his or her sense of self-esteem. When his or her sense of self-esteem is threatened, he or she is likely to become enraged. Therefore, narcissistic individuals seek out companions who reflect back their need for idolization and glorification so that they can maintain a stable self-image (Wells et al., 2006). Clearly, an individual with codependent characteristics fits this need. In fact, there is a natural attraction between individuals who struggle with issues of codependency and those who display narcissistic traits (Agrawal, Narayanan, & Oltmanns, 2013).

Case Example for Attraction to Narcissism

Ani and Charlie have come for couples counseling, stating that they are having trouble communicating and wish to discuss this struggle in the hopes of improving their ability to support each other. Ani is a 36-year-old first-generation Chinese American female. Having emigrated from China as a very small child,

Ani grew up as a citizen of the United States. Charlie is a second-generation Chinese American, having been born and raised in the United States. As they begin to discuss their struggles within the initial session, it is established that while Ani had been asking Charlie to attend counseling with her for several years, it was not until Ani threatened to leave the marriage that Charlie agreed to give counseling a try. In fact, once he agreed to this, he insisted on finding the therapist himself and making the first appointment.

Charlie and Ani have been married for 12 years and have two daughters, ages 10 and 8. They both report being highly involved and committed parents. In fact, Ani states that her desire to seek counseling at this time is because she wants to do everything within her power to maintain the current family structure for the sake of her children.

As sessions continue, the counselor notices that every time she attempts to engage with Ani, Charlie quickly responds. When the counselor points this out, Charlie becomes angry and defensive, stating, "I am only trying to help. Ani does not always see things correctly." As the counselor gently challenges Charlie in order to attempt to facilitate a discussion where both parties are free to participate, Charlie responds with an increasingly intense level of anger and becomes more and more agitated. At the same time, the counselor notices that Ani seems to become increasingly withdrawn and solicitous, making excuses for Charlie and attempting to diffuse the level of tension in the room. She explains to the counselor that Charlie is just tired; he had a hard week at work and is not sleeping well.

Reflection

In working with this couple, the counselor is likely to conceptualize this relationship as one in which Charlie is dominant and Ani seems to accommodate Charlie's mood fluctuations. In addition, the counselor is likely to notice Charlie's tendency to continually control sessions, attempting to ensure that the focus of the content is on him and his needs—signs of narcissism. In response to Charlie's reactions, Ani appears to become more and more solicitous. As Charlie's attention reverts more and more specifically to himself and his needs, Ani's attention seems to follow, becoming increasingly focused on Charlie and his needs.

As the sessions continue, the counselor asks to see Ani and Charlie individually in order to assess where each of them is regarding their perception of their relationship. In the session with Charlie, the counselor begins to more clearly identify the narcissistic tendencies evident within his personality. Charlie is adamant that he is perfectly happy. He loves Ani. He loves his children. He is, however, concerned about Ani, sharing that he does not understand why she is always so unhappy. As the counselor attempts to assist Charlie in considering Ani's needs, Charlie responds with, "She doesn't have any needs. We have plenty of money. I go to work every day. I come home every night. I have never cheated on her. She is lucky to have me." When the counselor continues to push by suggesting that perhaps it is difficult for Charlie to truly listen and hear Ani, Charlie storms out, stating that the counseling is a waste of time. Clearly, the counselor is unable to get it and unable to help.

In the session with Ani, the counselor is struck by Ani's obvious anxiety. In probing, the counselor finds that Ani has come to this session in opposition to Charlie's wishes. He did not want her to attend, as he had decided that this was a waste of time. As the session progresses, it becomes clear that Ani's primary focus revolves around keeping Charlie happy.

As she begins to discuss her past, Ani shares that she grew up as the oldest daughter of an alcoholic mother. She reports that most of her childhood was spent worrying about what might erupt at home and working very hard to take care of everything within her power to facilitate a sense of calm and predictability. When the counselor probes to see how Ani's needs were met, she is unable to respond to this and is even unable to identify what she wants and needs now. The counselor encourages Ani to continue within the counseling relationship, stating that perhaps she can work on developing her sense of self and self-worth. Ani agrees to this and makes an appointment to follow up with the counselor.

Implications for the Counselor

In this case, the counselor might begin to formulate a narcissistic personality disorder diagnosis for Charlie. In all of the sessions with Charlie to date, he presents as domineering, self-absorbed, and unable even to consider Ani's feelings or needs. Given Charlie's refusal to commit to the counseling process, the counselor is left with Ani as an individual client.

Ani presents as codependent. Therefore, in working with Ani, it will be important to work toward gaining her trust. Once a therapeutic alliance has been established and the relationship between Ani and the counselor is such that Ani begins to value the insight the counselor might offer, the counselor can begin to facilitate discussions regarding Ani's childhood experiences. These conversations might be useful in helping Ani make the connection between her childhood and her present-day attraction to individuals who are not respectful of her. It might also be beneficial to investigate other relationships in Ani's life in order to determine if this attraction occurs in other arenas.

In this case, the counselor might consider a goal of assisting Ani to become aware of her own needs and feelings. Once this awareness has been established, the counselor might work with Ani to investigate why she has difficulty considering her own needs as important in her closest relationships. Finally, the counselor might wish to explore Ani's attraction to individuals who are unable to meet her needs.

Discussion Questions

1. Do you agree that Charlie has displayed characteristics associated with a diagnosis of narcissistic personality disorder? Why or why not?
2. How do you make sense of the fact that Ani does not appear to see Charlie's behavior as inappropriate?
3. How is this situation linked to Ani's experience of being raised by a mother with an AUD?

Inability to Create or Maintain an Authentic Self

I have already discussed the construct of identity development within the context of living with an individual with an SUD. In essence, the development of a stable and healthy self-image can be thwarted in a number of ways when this development is occurring in an environment where the substance abuse of another individual has become a central and organizing feature (Arnold & Fisch, 2011). On a related note, the authentic expression of the self has been linked to self-esteem and overall psychological well-being (Heppner et al., 2008). In other words, individuals with higher levels of self-esteem generally report a level of comfort in presenting what they consider their authentic selves to the world. They do not feel the need to hide parts of themselves, and they do not worry excessively about how their authentic self will be perceived or received.

Carl Rogers defined *self-concept* as consisting of three distinct components: self-image, self-esteem, and ideal self (Rogers, 1961). *Self-image* refers to how an individual perceives him- or herself, on the basis of specific attributes. For example, one's perception of one's physical appearance would comprise a portion of that individual's self-image. *Self-esteem* is a more global evaluation of the self and refers to the sense of value individuals assign to themselves. Self-esteem tends to change over time, depending on what an individual uses to assess his or her value. Finally, Roger defined the *ideal self* as the self an individual aspires to be. Although this portion of the self-concept will change over time, it tends to be fixed at any given moment in a person's ongoing development. According to Rogers, *authenticity* refers to an individuals' openness to experience and the uncensored expression of their experience. For example, authentic individuals will not close off parts of themselves in the midst of a painful situation. Nor will they necessarily refrain from sharing their authentic and genuine feelings. If an authentic person is in a situation that evokes anger for them, they will not turn away from the anger; they will experience it.

In turn, they may share that anger in an attempt to resolve it, rather than stuff it or pretend they are not angry.

An individual with a strong sense of identity would also be well differentiated, which means he or she is able to control emotional reactivity through the use of appropriate boundaries. On the other hand, someone lacking self-identity would be easily influenced by others and have trouble making his or her own decisions. Identity of self begins to develop in childhood and can be affected by one's surroundings, including social and family environments. Therefore, individuals who grow up in substance-abusing families may have difficulties expressing their authentic selves (Liota, 2012).

Case Example for Inability to Create or Maintain an Authentic Self
• • •

Calvin, an 18-year-old Jamaican male, has sought counseling where he attends college because of a recent dispute with his female partner, Rebecca. Calvin is a first-generation college student and grew up in a large family as the oldest child. He is currently in his first semester of college and reports feelings of anxiety and stress. Calvin has never been in counseling but claims that he has been consistently sad and decided that counseling may be helpful at this point.

Calvin eventually discloses more information regarding his relationship with Rebecca. He reports feeling panicked because she does not want to spend as much time together lately, and she recently told him that they need time apart. Rebecca has expressed concern regarding Calvin's lack of a support system beyond her. Calvin feels they do not spend enough time together.

Calvin attributes most of his sadness to this current dispute and would like to talk about ways to work through this problem. He claims that what he really wants is to figure out how to get Rebecca to want to spend more time with him, stating that he feels empty when he is not with her. His reaction to his anxiety is to frantically attempt to figure out what Rebecca might want or what might make her more inclined to want to spend time with him. When the counselor attempts to explore his interests and support system beyond Rebecca, Calvin reports that these things do not exist for him. When the counselor probes in order to determine what brings Calvin joy, Calvin is unable to respond.

Reflection

At this point, the counselor might be observing some of Calvin's underlying issues, which include an intense desire to control the level of closeness he has with Rebecca. This intense desire may relate to an inability to individuate from others, especially Rebecca. His story thus far might lead the counselor to wonder if Calvin is struggling with his own identity, as it appears that he is relying on Rebecca to provide a sense of security. It also seems as though Calvin's identity exists exclusively through his relationship with Rebecca.

After further probing, Calvin discloses more about his upbringing and earlier family life. He is the oldest of six children. He has one brother and four sisters. For as long as Calvin can remember, his father was an alcoholic. Calvin has very few memories of his dad being sober. Calvin also reports that his father was physically and verbally abusive; Calvin took the brunt of this abuse to protect his siblings. Calvin shared that his mother left when he was 9 to escape the abuse and in doing so abandoned him and his siblings.

Calvin reports that after his mother left, his father's drinking increased and he became more aggressive. Calvin shares stories about not wanting to bring any friends home in fear of how his father might act in front of them. Calvin often refers to himself as never being good enough or loveable. He remembers blaming himself for his mother's leaving, feeling that if he could have interceded with his father in a more productive manner, his mother might have stayed. At the same time, Calvin remembers times of fury regarding his mother's leaving, reporting that he generally felt either intense guilt or intense rage.

As counseling progresses, Calvin and the counselor begin to explore his identity as a child and an adolescent. Calvin is initially confused by this topic, stating that he never really thought about himself. He was so preoccupied with protecting himself and his siblings that he never remembers a time when he daydreamed or thought about who he was and what he might become. During adolescence, Calvin was forced to hold down a job and was simultaneously determined to maintain his grades so that he could go to college. In terms of relationships, Calvin remembers always becoming extremely attached to people. He constantly feared abandonment by both friends and romantic partners. In response to this fear, Calvin reports that his tendency was to work very hard to figure out what the other person wanted and attempt to provide that. Even though this response seemed to push people away, Calvin was unable to break this pattern. He reports having his heart broken repeatedly, reinforcing his notion of himself as unlovable.

Calvin and the counselor agree that one of the goals of counseling should address Calvin's lack of a well-defined, separate identity that he might be able to authentically maintain within his relationships. As they continue to explore Calvin's past, they focus on attempting to access any feelings Calvin may have had regarding himself in the world.

Implications for the Counselor

Calvin demonstrates an inability to maintain a sense of self that is separate in his relationships with others. This pattern has repeatedly led to failed relationships and to Calvin constantly feeling abandoned.

Again, the counselor will begin working with Calvin by establishing a relationship in which he can feel a sense of security and the freedom to honestly explore these issues.

In this case, Calvin reveals that his inability to create an authentic identity is directly related to growing up in an alcoholic family. His father's drinking and abuse prohibited Calvin from meeting the typical developmental milestones. Once the counselor has established a therapeutic alliance with Calvin, they may begin to use techniques to encourage Calvin to explore his identity. For example, the counselor may begin this process by helping Calvin identify activities and people he is drawn to, encouraging him to engage with some of these. The counselor might also attempt to use a cognitive approach in an effort to challenge some of Calvin's thinking. Finally, the counselor might work toward challenging Calvin to change his behavior in relationships, even at those times that the panic sets in. The counselor can provide a space for releasing and exploring the panic and anxiety that Calvin feels in relationships, in an effort to discourage him from acting out these feelings within his close relationships.

Discussion Questions

1. How do you conceptualize Calvin's intense attachment in his relationship with Rebecca?
2. In what ways might this issue relate to Calvin's childhood experiences?
3. Do you agree that a lack of a clear identity is at the root of Calvin's current struggles?
4. How might you begin to explore these issues with Calvin?

Chapter 9

Behavioral Consequences of Living With a Person With an SUD

In addition to the emotional and relational issues associated with living with a family member with an SUD, several potential behavioral consequences have been identified (see Table 8). For example, the ability to self-regulate the intensity of one's emotional responses is a skill that is expected throughout adulthood. For every adult, situations and experiences will arise that trigger emotional responses. Adults are expected to control their emotional responses and express feelings with restraint and in a manner appropriate to the emotion-producing situation. The skills associated with emotion regulation are developed throughout childhood and across the developmental stages.

Issues With Self-Regulation/Acting Out

For children who live with a substance-abusing family member, there is an increased risk for having issues associated with a limited ability to emotionally self-regulate. In fact, young COAs display higher rates of externalized behavior problems, and COAs in general have been shown to exhibit higher levels of acting-out behavior than children whose parents do not have an AUD (Eiden, Edwards, & Leonard, 2007). Differences in brain circuitry between the COAs and children of nonalcoholics have also been noted. In a study of impulse

Table 8
Behavioral Consequences of Living With an Individual Struggling With an SUD

Consequence	Description
Problems with self-regulation	Inability to self-regulate the intensity of emotional response; lower levels of impulse control
Self-destructive behavior/acting out	Potentially higher levels of acting out behavior
Substance use/abuse	Increased vulnerability to substance use/abuse

Note. SUD = substance use disorder.

control circuitry comparing COAs with children of nonalcoholics, significant differences were found between the two groups (Hardee et al., 2014). By adolescence, the COA group had developed circuitry that interfered with their ability to inhibit responses to emotionally charged situations. In other studies, COAs have been shown to exhibit significantly different behavioral responses than children of nonalcoholics (Klostermann et al., 2011). To be specific, COAs were more prone to venting emotions than children of nonalcoholics, and they displayed significantly higher levels of vulnerability to poor self-regulation (Adkinson et al., 2013). Ultimately, children of parents with an SUD are at higher risk of criminal behavior and delinquency (Obot & Anthony, 2004).

Case Example for Issues With
Self-Regulation/Acting Out
• • •

Mya, a 16-year-old high school junior, has come for counseling. Mya has a history of acting out at home and in school, and so private counseling has been recommended for several years. Although Mya is resistant to the idea, her mother, Alicia, has decided that participation in counseling is no longer optional.

Most recently, Mya initiated a physical altercation with a classmate. This incident took place at the end of a typical school day. According to the school counselor, Mya insisted that the other involved student had been talking behind her back and ultimately glanced at Mya in a way she experienced as threatening. As the two students were leaving school for the day, Mya tripped the other student. When the student fell to the ground, Mya kicked her in the upper thigh. Upon seeing the incident, a nearby teacher positioned himself between both girls. Mya allegedly went into a rage and began threatening the teacher. When she lunged toward the teacher who was attempting to intervene, two additional teachers approached and held Mya by both arms. The teachers continued to restrain Mya, and the in-school peace officer was summoned. When she arrived on the scene, the officer was able to calm the situation to a point where Mya willingly went to the office. At this point, Mya's mother was called and summoned to the school. The final result of this incident included Mya and her mother agreeing to enter therapy in exchange for a delay in pursuing a legal solution to the incident.

In the first counseling session, the counselor meets jointly with Mya and her mother, Alicia. Upon inquiring about the nature of the concerns that brought Mya into counseling, the counselor is immediately aware that Alicia appears to be under the influence of alcohol. In fact, the counselor can smell the alcohol as Alicia describes Mya's consistently bad behavior.

After the counselor gets the needed information from Alicia and asks her to step out of the room, Mya seems reluctant and quiet. She is also clearly angry. When the counselor asks her to talk about the incident that had transpired, Mya is quick to blame the other student for the incident that led to this appointment. In addition, she repeatedly refers to her mother as "the drunk" and states that she (Alicia) should be the one getting help. When the counselor asks Mya to elaborate on this, Mya reports that she cannot remember the last time her mother was sober when she returned home from school. Mya, as the youngest of three children, is the only child still living at home with her unmarried mother. Mya claims that she sees her siblings very rarely, as her 26-year-old bother is a "junkie," and her 20-year-old sister is in college and thinks she is better than Mya.

Reflection

At this point, the counselor is likely beginning to link Mya's history of acting out with issues within the family. The counselor has observed Alicia as intoxicated, and this has been validated by Mya's account. Conceptualizing this case within the context of a family unit that includes alcoholism might lead the counselor to consider the impact of this situation on Mya's behavior.

In working with Mya further, the counselor is slowly able to gain a modicum of Mya's trust and begins to push her to make the connection between her behavior and her life circumstances. When Mya does this, the counselor begins to gently push Mya to consider who she is hurting most by dealing with her painful circumstances by continually getting into trouble. As the work progresses, the counselor is able to help Mya consider her own future. Mya, in an embarrassed tone, reveals that she has always loved animals, but she also reports that she knows she is not smart enough to become a veterinarian. However, she has always thought about working in some capacity where she has contact with animals. Up to this point, Mya has only thought about these ideas and has never told anyone, much less considered making some kind of plan to realize this desire. In fact, Mya claims that she has not even begun to consider what she will do upon leaving high school. At this point, the counselor and Mya agree to continue considering the future and simultaneously process and deal with Mya's present reality.

Implications for the Counselor

The case of Mya is complex and difficult. There are immediate concerns and implicit goals, and there is a history and a future to integrate in order to facilitate a long-term positive outcome. The counselor will likely focus right away on assisting Mya in figuring out how she can avoid getting herself into additional trouble. Given Mya's history, the counselor is likely to address any risky behavior first. In addition, the counselor may want to assist Mya in better understanding the potential consequences of continuing to act out. At the same time, developmentally and systemically, Mya is extremely vulnerable to continuing the destructive pattern she has adopted. The additional issue of living with a mother who has an AUD complicates the counseling relationship. The counselor may need to be directive and provide continual reality checks. However, the development of a trusting and safe relationship must be simultaneously established. Therefore, the counselor is likely to use a combination of rapport building and more directive cognitive and behavioral approaches with Mya. The use of pieces of motivational interviewing (described in detail in Chapter 11) may also be indicated and helpful in structuring an approach that might facilitate this balance.

In working with Mya, the goals are diverse. The concrete goal of working toward alternative ways to cope with frustration and pain that do not result in Mya's compromising her record are important and immediate. In addition, the counselor might be considering more long-range goals. These goals might include identifying aspirations and making plans to realize them and working toward learning about healthy relationships and how to go about facilitating them.

Discussion Questions

1. What do you think Mya is attempting to achieve through acting out?
2. Do you believe that Mya's acting out is related to her mother's drinking? In what ways?
3. How would you balance needing to be directive with Mya with establishing a trusting therapeutic relationship?

Substance Use/Abuse

Finally, in terms of potential behavioral consequences of living with an individual with an SUD, perhaps the most obvious is that these individuals are at an increased risk of developing a substance abuse problem themselves. In fact, the prevalence of substance abuse among COAs is consistently higher than among children of nonalcoholics

(Devine, 2013; Kopera et al., 2014; Mersky, 2008, Park & Schepp, 2014), and parental substance abuse is one of the most frequently cited predictors for the development of an SUD (Bailey & Stewart, 2014; Wilens, Yule, Martelon, Zulauf, & Faraone, 2014). Medical and scientific researchers are investigating the possible neurobiological connections to this phenomenon, including genetic factors that may contribute to an increased risk of developing an SUD (Agrawal & Lynskey, 2014; Matto, Brown, & Ballan, 2014). In addition, there is evidence that COAs may possess a cognitive processing bias that predisposes them to thinking differently than children of nonalcoholics about the use of illicit substances. To be specific, there is tentative evidence that a covert cognitive processing bias might exist for COAs that partially explains the intergenerational transmission of addictive behaviors (Belles, Budde, Moesgen, & Klein, 2011).

Instead of presenting a case to illustrate this particular issue, I explore possible protocols for serving this population of clients. Initially, it is incumbent upon counselors to maintain an awareness of the increased risk of a substance abuse issue when working with any client who has lived or is currently living with someone with an SUD. This awareness includes assessing that client's substance use behavior and attending to content that might indicate an increase in substance use. In the event that counselors find themselves working with an individual who has an untreated SUD, it is likely that a referral for substance-abuse-specific treatment is indicated. In fact, it is not uncommon for counselors to insist on such treatment prior to individual counseling in an outpatient setting, and best practices within the field of substance abuse indicate that an individual with an SUD should be treated for that disorder before working on other issues that may exist for the client (Brooks & McHenry, 2015). Therefore, in terms of protocol, access to a comprehensive and up-to-date listing of facilities that offer both inpatient and outpatient treatment for substance abuse is imperative.

In the case of counselors who work in settings that allow for psychoeducational programming to exist (i.e., schools, colleges, community mental health facilities), prevention programs can be initiated. By running groups or providing educational programs for clients who live with an individual with an SUD, counselors can provide a vehicle for supporting this population of clients. Group counseling is covered in more detail in Chapter 11. However, several resources for how to run such groups are listed here.

Resources to Support People Living With an Individual With an SUD

American Academy for Child and Adolescent Psychiatry. (2011). *Facts for families.* Retrieved from http://www.aacap.org/App_Themes/ AACAP/docs/facts_for_families/17_children_of_alcoholics.pdf

National Association for Children of Alcoholics (NACoA). (2001). *Children of alcoholics: A kit for educators* (4th ed.). Retrieved from http://www.nacoa.org/pdfs/EDkit_web_06.pdf

Nemours Center for Childrens Health Media (TeensHealth). (n.d.). *Coping with an alcoholic parent.* Retrieved from http://kidshealth. org/teen/drug_alcohol/alcohol/coping_alcoholic.html

Substance Abuse and Mental Health Services Administration (SAMHSA). (2004). *Children of alcoholics: A community action guide.* Retrieved from https://store.samhsa.gov/shin/content/MS939/MS939.pdf

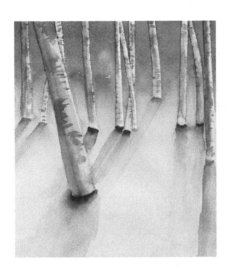

Chapter 10

Multicultural Considerations

We counselors know that SUD crosses all known boundaries (i.e., gender, socioeconomic status, race, ethnicity, sexual orientation). Although this fact is true and important to recognize, it is equally important to consider the differences you will encounter when you work with families who have a member struggling with an SUD. Counselors are trained to competently counsel individuals from a multicultural perspective, and this extends to working with substance-abusing families. Issues related to a client's cultural background must be integrated into the conceptualization and treatment for any client struggling with an SUD in the family.

The counseling profession has made an explicit commitment to competently work with all clients, regardless of socioeconomic status, ethnicity, race, or sexual orientation. This commitment has been supported through the development and endorsement of a set of multicultural competencies that guide our work with clients from all backgrounds (Sue, Arrendondo, & McDavis, 1992). As professionals with a commitment to optimal development across the human life span, counselors are expected to competently facilitate work on cultural identity. In fact, cultural identity plays an important role in mediating both the issues clients present with and the resiliency they bring to their capacity to cope with these issues (Fawcett, 2012). This chapter covers some of the multicultural considerations in working with clients with a substance-abusing family member.

Socioeconomic Diversity

We are all aware of the significant range in socioeconomic circumstances within our country, and this diversity will most likely be reflected in the population of clients we serve. In the case of work in the area of substance abuse, this vast socioeconomic spread will significantly affect treatment. Right now, insurance companies are reluctant to pay for residential substance abuse treatment. The trend is to provide hospitalizations for a short period of time for the purposes of detoxification (i.e., detox). Once a client has gone through detox, he or she is generally referred for outpatient care. This care may be in the form of a structured outpatient treatment program or via a referral for individual counseling service. Often, this treatment is ineffective, and in the event that a client seems to require an intensive residential treatment setting, the client may be left to his or her own financial devises. The premier residential treatment centers cost in excess of $30,000 for a one-month stay (the typical amount of time suggested). This cost has created a serious dilemma regarding access to treatment—a dilemma that has yet to be solved. Therefore, cost often prohibits all but the most financially able clients from accessing residential treatment, creating a scenario in which only a specific segment of the population will receive these services. Although treatment centers across the country have attempted to meet the needs of the remainder of individuals struggling with an SUD and their families, most professionals in the field of addictions know that we continue to face a serious deficit in terms of the services we are able to provide.

On a related note, McGoldrick, Giordano, and Garcia-Preto (2005), in their book on ethnicity and family therapy, emphasized the disillusionment and frustration generated by persistent poverty and oppression, and they linked these conditions to a high rate of drug and alcohol abuse among the poor. We therefore face a situation in which we are often not able to provide the best services to the clients most in need. Our poorest citizens lack access to the kinds of services necessary to sustain sobriety.

Race and Ethnicity

One of the significant differences related to race and ethnicity with a profound impact on substance abuse treatment is that of stress. To be specific, differences exist in sources of stress and sources of resiliency for particular groups of clients. For this reason, it is important to consider these and other factors in the treatment of family members of substance abusers. For example, compared with White people, Black people experience a greater number of negative stressful events. In addition, the two groups are likely to differ in how they experience different types of stressors and in the types of coping strategies used in response to those stressors (Hoggard, Byrd, & Sellers, 2012).

They also derive social support, a buffer against stress, from different sources. For example, Black and Latino adolescents are more likely than their White counterparts to be the victim of, or witness to, violence; to experience the death of a parent or sibling; to be involved in the criminal justice system; and to have parents whose income has recently decreased (Gayman, Cislo, Goidel, & Ueno, 2014). An additional and important source of stress for all non-White clients is racism, which has been shown to increase feelings of anger, hostility, alienation, and helplessness. All of these feelings have been associated with negative health outcomes (Anderson, 2013), including the use and abuse of illicit substances.

Thus, it may be that substance use and abuse serves different functions across racial and ethnic groups. Minority clients may be more likely to use drugs to "anesthetize" the emotional effects of racism, poverty, oppression, and lack of opportunity (Crawford et al., 2013). Substance abuse among White youth, on the other hand, appears to be tied to peer use and abuse. These facts point to differential interventions that take into account these cultural differences.

Recent studies have suggested that a youth's identification with his or her own ethnic culture is not in itself a factor related to drug use or abuse but instead can serve as protective in association with other factors known to have an impact on resiliency (Castro & Alarcon, 2002). Thus, counselors should address cultural identity with both substance abusers and their families during the counseling process. However, the evidence suggests that this is the piece of the treatment puzzle that is often ignored or minimized. Oetting and Beauvais (1990) pointed this fact out quite some time ago. In fact, they suggested that cultural recovery be integrated in the substance abuse treatment process. They described cultural recovery as regaining an ethnic identity and acquiring a support network committed to the person's recovery. In addition, they suggested that making a religious, spiritual, or moral recommitment and gaining a social role in a recovering community, society at large, or both are important factors in providing treatment that is sustained. Those individuals who fail to make a satisfactory cultural recovery are at risk for relapse, as the reintegration back into their specific community must be supported in order to minimize the chances of slipping back into the behavioral and social patterns that were closely associated with drug or alcohol use. Although the research on this topic is directed at the substance abuser, it is assumed that the family will require the same kinds of resources in order to both support the substance abuser's recovery and sustain their own mental health and recovery.

One of the issues discussed within the literature on treating diverse populations for SUD is that of access to treatment. Access to treatment is viewed as multidimensional, encompassing psychological and sociological access as well as physical access. For example, staff composition is critical in treating families with a substance-abusing member, particularly in initiating treatment and in retaining clients. To be specific, diversity among treatment providers or members of treatment teams is essential. The provision of treatment providers who look like or have attributes clients can directly relate to affects commitment and willingness to stay in treatment. In fact, in one study, Abbott and Chase (2008) found that individuals did not seek alcohol or drug treatment from a local program because the program did not have staff that included members of their ethnic group. On a related note, physical access to treatment is critical. It is important to locate treatment facilities in easily accessible geographic areas. Oftentimes substance abusers and their families are unable to travel in order to access treatment, or they are unwilling to be treated in communities that are significantly different from those in which they reside. Providing treatment that is located within neighborhoods where individuals reside increases the likelihood of sustained recovery.

Black Clients

For Black clients, it has been suggested that core cultural values be considered and assessed at the start of substance abuse treatment. These values include such things as communalism, religion/spirituality, expressiveness, respect for verbal communication skills, connection to ancestors and history, commitment to family, and intuition and experience versus empiricism (Resnicow, Soler, Braithwaite, Selassie, & Smith, 1999). African culture has been characterized by a unique sense of time, a communication style that might emphasize oral forms of communication such as storytelling, the inclusion of religious or spiritual themes, and historical references (Hecht, Collier, & Ribeau, 1993). If Black clients adopt this cultural attribute, several treatment implications arise. For example, the use of print in traditional substance abuse treatment (i.e., Alcoholics Anonymous) is highly regarded and does not generally include historical references or information that might be specific to particular cultural groups. However, the use of storytelling and a spiritual focus are also highly valued within the 12-step model. Sensitivity to a particular client and his or her family is essential in providing the supports that best suit their individual needs and worldview.

Latina/o Clients

In several community-based studies investigating alcohol use among various ethnicities, it was found that Latino men have significantly higher rates of alcohol consumption than Latinas. In addition, Latinos were more likely to experience greater physical and social consequences compared with their male White peers (Rojas, Hallford, Brand, & Tivis 2012). Therefore, the identification of treatment modalities and techniques that are effective with the Latino population is essential.

For Latino individuals, a set of core cultural values has been elaborated. These include the following: *familismo* (importance of family), *respeto* (respect for elders), *dignidad* (the value of self-worth), *caridad* (the value of rituals and ceremonies), fatalism, and *simpatía* (the importance of positive social interactions). In order to explore these themes, it has been suggested that the novella format (i.e., the use of stories) be considered, as the storytelling aspect of treatment may effect the greatest change for Latino clients (Lalonde, Rabinowitz, Shefsky, & Washienko, 1997). Again, highlighting this aspect of the 12-step recovery model might make sense for this group of clients. In addition, integrating the family into the recovery process in an intentional manner and creating a recovery community that includes other Latino individuals may result in a greater likelihood of sustained recovery.

Asian/Pacific Islander Clients

National surveys suggest that Asian Americans have a lower alcohol use prevalence compared with other racial groups (Substance Abuse & Mental Health Services Administration [SAMHSA], n.d.). However, more current research suggests that the incidence of reported problems related to alcohol and drug use among Asian Americans may not be reflective of the actual state of alcohol problems among this population (Cheng, Lee, & Iwamoto, 2012). In addition, Asian Americans report higher levels of depression when compared with other ethnic groups (Young, Fang, & Zisook, 2010), and, as discussed earlier, depression and substance use and abuse are linked.

In terms of treatment, according to the SAMHSA (n.d.), the rate of substance abuse treatment admissions among Asian Americans and Pacific Islanders has increased dramatically. Furthermore, compelling evidence suggests that Asian American heavy drinkers experience a higher rate of negative consequences compared with heavy drinkers of other ethnicities (Park, Shibusawa, Yoon, & Son, 2010). Despite this fact, Asian Americans and Pacific Islanders are not as likely as other groups to access treatment. Cognitive, affective, value orientation, and physical barriers have been identified as factors contributing to the underuse of mental health services by Asian Americans, despite the consequences they may face as a result of their drug or alcohol use (Goebert & Nishimura, 2011). Asian Americans tend to consider addiction to be a private matter. In addition, Asian American and Pacific Islander clients who did seek help received fewer total services within their treatment programs, and they exhibited significantly more negative attitudes toward treatment when compared with non-Asian American and Pacific Islanders (Niv, Wong, & Hser, 2007).

Clients of Middle Eastern Descent

It is uncommon for an individual of Middle Eastern descent to seek help outside of the family, even for a problem related to the use of drugs and alcohol. For those people of Middle Eastern descent who are Muslim, the Islamic concept of *ummah,* or community, discourages Muslims from seeking treatment for emotional or mental health issues (Dwairy, 2006). Although there is a primary focus and reliance on the family for support and direction within the Middle Eastern culture, even family therapy may not be welcomed, as this may be considered antithetical to cultural norms (McGoldrick et al., 2005). The shame associated with participating in a behavior that is theologically and culturally deemed as sinful may also keep Middle Eastern individuals, including Americans of Middle Eastern descent, from seeking treatment. It is therefore assumed among treatment providers that substance use and abuse is underreported among this particular group.

There is limited research that examines treatment for clients of Middle Eastern descent. However, it has been suggested that if either a Christian or Muslim Middle Eastern client were to reach out for assistance, the 12-step model might be well suited to their treatment needs. The reliance on a Higher Power may appeal to individuals who are already seeking spiritual guidance on a regular basis. In addition, the solidarity that exists in programs such as Alcoholics Anonymous (AA) is consistent with Islamic law. The construct of the ummah refers directly to a collective consciousness around a common struggle, a notion that is central to the 12-step model. Despite these intuitive connections, however, one study did indicate that the use of 12-step programs among substance abusers of Middle Eastern descent was not as effective as a more comprehensive treatment program. The comprehensive treatment referred to in this study included individual, group, and family therapy and the use of psychopharmacological interventions when indicated (Abdel-Mawgoud, Fateem, & Al-Sharif, 1995).

Native American Clients

It is widely accepted that the Native American population has been disproportionately affected by substance use and abuse (Legha, Raleigh-Cohn, Fickenscher, & Novins, 2014). Although the reasons for this disproportionate effect are not completely understood, cultural conditions and differences are thought to play a significant role. Traditional treatment efforts have not been effective for this population of clients. In response to this failure, more tribal-centric treatment has been suggested. However, such barriers as funding and access to treatment have been cited as obstacles that have not yet been overcome (Eitle & Eitle, 2014).

Sexual Orientation

In every study comparing substance use and abuse between lesbian, gay, transgender, and queer (LGBTQ) adolescents and non-LGBTQ adolescents, the LGBTQ group is shown to have higher rates of use.

Researchers have offered several explanations for this phenomenon. First, sexual minority teens may use drugs and alcohol as a tool to rationalize their feelings and behavior (Chaney & Brubaker, 2012). Other explanations include the use of social learning models to explain these differences. For example, the LGBTQ communities have often historically been centered on activities that involve drinking and drug use (e.g., bars, circuit parties). In addition, the expectations and perceptions that drinking and drug use is normal in LGBTQ communities might increase the likelihood of LGBTQ individuals making the decision to drink or use drugs. Finally, the additional stress related to being a sexual minority could contribute to elevated substance use.

Meyer and Frost (2003) proposed a Minority Stress Model for understanding LGBTQ experiences in the context of stressors unique to that population. In fact, they explained the prevalence of mental health disorders in the LGBTQ population as caused at least partially by stigma-related social stressors. The two most commonly cited of these stressors are the importance of the bar scene in LGBTQ communities and sexual minority stress (including both discrimination and internalized homophobia; Hughes & Eliason, 2002).

In terms of treatment, there is little research on differential treatment outcomes for this population. However, increasing our understanding of treatment modalities that might benefit the LGBTQ community is especially important, as research has demonstrated that these clients enter treatment with more severe substance abuse problems than heterosexual clients (Cochran & Cauce, 2006). In addition, although the results of differences in the rate of alcoholism between heterosexual and gay men remains mixed (Green & Feinstein, 2012), there is evidence that lesbian and bisexual women seek treatment for alcohol use disorders more often than heterosexual women (Drabble, Trocki, Hughes, Korcha, & Lown, 2013).

Case Example for Multicultural Considerations
• • •

Carlos is a 15-year-old high school junior who has begun drinking and partying heavily. Currently at risk of not being promoted, Carlos has begun meeting on a regular basis with the school counselor.

Carlos is the oldest of four children, all of whom live with his biological parents, his aunt, and his paternal grandparents. His siblings include a 13-year-old sister, a 12-year-old sister, and an 8-year-old brother. Carlos is a first-generation American; his father and his grandparents are from Ecuador, and his mother is from Columbia. Carlos's parents met in the United States shortly after his mother arrived when she was 20. They have always lived in the same neighborhood, about a block away from the school.

Carlos is highly resistant to counseling initially, calling it "bullshit." He claims that he is fine and knows exactly what he is doing. He does not want to talk with anyone. Over time, however, Carlos begins to share his story. He reports that his family has always been poor. His father works as a janitor for a local office complex, and his mother has been cleaning houses ever since Carlos can remember. In fact, Carlos has picked up a job at a local grocery store in order to help out his family financially.

Carlos reports that he loved school when he was younger, and his records indicate that he was a very good student. He claims to have fantasies about going to college and getting his family "out of here." However, over time, he says these dreams evaporated, and Carlos began to feel as though he was destined to live out his days in the same neighborhood. He claims that this "is not so bad."

As this transition began to take place, Carlos reached the age where he became more interested in "hanging out with his friends." At first, they would simply hang around the neighborhood and talk. But as time went on, they began to drink. Carlos reports that he took to drinking immediately and began to look forward to "getting loaded." When he was introduced to marijuana, he claims that he felt as if he had hit the jackpot. He loved the way it made him feel. And because he was not even thinking about a future, he began to use either alcohol or marijuana virtually every day.

When Carlos shares information about his family, he reports that his father and his grandfather drink heavily. They frequently get together with some of the other men in the neighborhood and drink until well into the night. Because this drinking has never seemed to affect his father's ability to meet his responsibilities, Carlos does not see anything wrong with his father's drinking. It is the only fun his dad ever has. Carlos considers his family typical. They work hard and take care of their family. Carlos says that his family wants him to go to college, but they are not going to help him. They simply do not know how.

Reflection

Up to this point, the counselor might begin to assume that drinking and using marijuana has affected Carlos's level of motivation. It seems as though these behaviors were initiated at the same time that Carlos began to question his ability to create a different kind of life for himself.

When the counselor begins to probe regarding Carlos's personal and social life, Carlos seems to shut down. When the subject of intimate relationships comes up, Carlos deflects the conversation and talks initially about his friends' interest in girls. He emphatically insists that he is not interested in girls and just wants to continue to hang out with his friends. Eventually, however, Carlos discloses that he has actually been finding himself sexually attracted to his male friends. He says that he feels ashamed and does not know what is wrong with him. He states that he knows this is weird and wrong, and he knows that his family would never accept such a thing, but he does not know how to change these feelings. He asks the counselor to help him with this. To be specific, he wants the counselor to make him feel this kind of attraction to girls.

Implications for the Counselor

In the case of Carlos, the counselor will need to attend to a number of issues. From a developmental standpoint, Carlos is beginning to work on establishing an identity. He is tackling this developmental stage within the context of a family that has been struggling in a number of ways. The counselor will want to obtain an accurate picture of how Carlos has navigated previous developmental conflicts. In addition, Carlos is struggling with feelings of being attracted to males, and this attraction is extremely troublesome for him. So much so that Carlos has expressed his desire to change this fact. The counselor will need to approach this topic with a high level of sensitivity. Furthermore, it is essential in this case that the counselor gain a clear understanding of the cultural context in which Carlos is facing the issues he presents. To do so, the counselor must have an understanding of Carlos's cultural background and current cultural affiliations.

Discussion Questions

1. What do you see as the most critical issue for Carlos?
2. What are some of the multicultural considerations you might want to consider in working with Carlos?
3. How might you conceptualize the substance use issue in the context of these multicultural considerations?

Chapter 11

Treating Clients Living With a Person With an SUD

In previous chapters, I have addressed a variety of theoretical perspectives for conceptualizing the issues associated with living with a person who has an SUD. That is, I have described the application of family and developmental theories in the context of how these theories might apply to working with this population of clients. Likewise, I have looked at some of the specific consequences likely to result for individuals with a substance-abusing family member. The current chapter covers several specific theoretical orientations that can be applied to working with family members of substance abusers. In addition, several specific counseling modalities and strategies for working with this population of clients are discussed.

Applying Theory to Working With Families of Individuals With an SUD

Person-Centered Theory

The study of person-centered theory is foundational for professional counselors. Although person-centered theory is a distinct theoretical approach most closely associated with Carl Rogers, it has its roots in existentialism and humanistic psychology. Maslow (1969) was perhaps the original pioneer in the development of humanistic psychology, and he focused his work on the study of self-actualizing. Self-actualizing is characterized as a state of being in the world in which an individual has actualized his or her full human potential. Maslow suggested that humans strive for a state of self-actualization via a process whereby they seek to meet a series of needs, beginning with those most basic for survival. He proposed that motivation is driven by the extent to which these needs are met. Individuals who are hungry or homeless, for example, will be most strongly motivated to find food or shelter. When these basic needs are met, individuals will next strive to meet their need for safety, followed by an attempt to meet needs of belonging and love. Next, the individual will attempt to meet the need of esteem, both self-esteem and the esteem of others. When these preceding needs have been met, individuals will strive toward self-actualization, characterized by high levels of self-awareness, genuine caring, honesty, and autonomy.

In the case of individuals who live with a substance-abusing family member, it is not uncommon for them to feel that their safety needs have not been met; indeed, they may even struggle with fears regarding the meeting of their more basic needs (Hinrichs et al., 2011). In the event that such clients do feel that their safety needs have been met, they may continue to struggle with issues of love and belonging or issues of self-esteem. Consideration of Maslow's hierarchy of needs may benefit counselors working with this population as they begin to discern where a particular client is most vulnerable.

Rogers (1961) proposed that healing for clients takes place in the context of the relationship between the client and the counselor. In fact, person-centered theory endorses the need for a specific type of therapeutic relationship that facilitates change for a client. Rogers believed that if a set of "necessary and sufficient conditions" were present within the therapeutic relationship, the client would be propelled to discover his or her capacity for change. By being congruent, providing unconditional positive regard and acceptance, and conveying accurate empathy, the counselor can provide an environment in which a client can realize his or her individual potential for growth.

For clients who have lived with an individual who has an SUD, the establishment of such a relationship is essential. I have already discussed the issues of trust and self-esteem that can be at the very heart of the struggles such clients might be dealing with (Reyome et al., 2010). The establishment of a trusting and solid therapeutic relationship cannot be stressed enough, as this particular client population is likely to have experienced important relationships that did not meet their needs or contain the basic conditions so fundamental to healthy relationships. In addition, the therapeutic relationship, as described by Rogers, encourages a sense of empowerment. The belief in clients' ability to facilitate their own healing suggests a belief in their potential to facilitate change and growth. The combination of a consistent, trusting relationship and a genuine belief in the client's capacity for self-healing provides a foundation for growth essential for this population.

Cognitive Behavior Theories

A number of cognitive behavior theories have been applied to therapeutic work and are representative of theories that are at the heart of the counseling profession. CBT combines aspects of both cognitive and behavioral approaches and thus works on disrupting unhealthy thought patterns and changing and replacing behaviors that adversely affect overall psychological well-being (Corey, 2013). Although a number of theorists are credited with the development and exploration of cognitive approaches to therapy, Ellis (1994), Beck (1976), and Meichenbaum (1977) are perhaps the most well-known to counselors. Ellis (1994), a pioneer in the area of CBT, purported that emotional disturbance is the result of faulty or inaccurate beliefs that individuals hold about themselves, others, or situations. For example, a client may be upset to receive a reprimand from his or her boss. In examining the issue, the counselor and the client may discover that the client is in fact holding the belief that the boss now hates the client and the client will never be able to redeem himself or herself. Ellis would suggest that this belief is the cause of the emotional upset experienced by the client and would confront this belief in an effort to alter the client's thinking.

Beck (1976), like Ellis, believed that it is thinking that is at the root of emotional issues. Through his study of depression, Beck concluded that automatic thoughts and cognitive distortions are the specific triggers for emotional disturbance. He suggested that automatic thoughts (thoughts evoked in response to stimuli that trigger a seemingly automatic negative emotional response) and cognitive distortions (thinking about situations in a manner that does not fully represent the reality of the experience) are the cognitive conditions that lead to emotional discomfort and psychological upset. Oftentimes, automatic thoughts and cognitive distortions occur as the result of a present-day experience triggering an emotional response from the past. A client might automatically engage in thinking that supports a view of reality that is not accurate, because of the triggering of an emotional response to similar situations from his or her past. A client who has lived with a substance-abusing family member could, for example, conclude that his or her partner has a substance abuse problem after a single episode of excessive drinking that is, in fact, highly uncharacteristic of that individual.

Finally, Meichenbaum (1977) suggested a theory of cognitive behavior modification that focuses on assisting clients in changing self-verbalizations. According to Meichenbaum, the self-statements that individuals make lead to behavior patterns that cause psychic pain.

He believes that clients need to examine how they think and behave in order to interrupt the destructive patterns that have developed. An example with a client who has lived with a substance-abusing family member might be a case where an individual seems to continuously sabotage important relationships. This sabotaging may occur because the person makes self-statements or carries on an internal dialogue that reinforces that he or she is unlovable or unworthy of love (thoughts such as, "As soon as this person sees what I am really like, he or she will abandon me"). These thoughts are likely to lead the client to behave in ways that cause distance in the relationship and ultimately destroy it.

According to the NIDA (2012a), CBT is endorsed as an evidence-based treatment option for working with individuals struggling with an SUD. CBT is generally adapted for use with substance-abusing individuals as a means of assisting clients in the development of coping strategies. To be specific, clients are taught to identify triggers and situations likely to induce cravings, and develop strategies that can be used to manage these situations. Evidence suggests that the use of such strategies results in long-term benefits, as the skills that clients learn through CBT remain beyond the completion of the therapy (Carroll et al., 2005; DeVito, Babuscio, Nich, Ball, & Carroll, 2014).

In addition, CBTs have also been shown to be effective in working with families (Dattilio, 2010). Many of the larger residential treatment programs for individuals with SUD in the United States include an extensive family program that incorporates the use of CBTs (Caron Foundation, n.d.; Hazeldon Betty Ford Foundation, n.d.-a). These programs generally provide group counseling for parents, children, siblings, and other family members affected by the substance use of another. Support is provided to the family in the form of psychoeducational group sessions and the exploration of coping strategies for adjusting to the sobriety of the substance-abusing family member.

When using CBT with family members of individuals struggling with an SUD, a counselor might consider assisting the client in identifying specific thoughts and behaviors that result in negative consequences for the client. The client and counselor can then work toward developing alternative coping strategies that can be used in dealing with those issues. For example, if a client expresses an inability to assert himself or herself, this inability could be explored in the context of CBT. The counselor and the client might begin by discerning the precise thoughts associated with the client's lack of assertiveness. Maybe in a situation where the client wants to assert himself or herself, the client thinks, "I am not allowed to express myself in an effort to meet my own needs." This thought could be replaced with a thought such as, "It is fine, and in fact healthy, for me to assertively express my own needs." Alternative ways of thinking can be explored, and the client can practice responding internally with these new thoughts. Finally, the client and counselor could work to identify specific scenarios in which the client wished to be more assertive. The client and the counselor could then collaboratively develop new strategies for coping with such scenarios that the client could practice.

Group Counseling

Group counseling has been endorsed as a primary modality for working with individuals with an SUD (Brooks & McHenry, 2015). In fact, it is used more frequently and with higher levels of success than individual counseling with this population of clients (Fiorentine, 2001; MacGowan, 2006). Because group counseling has become the treatment modality most frequently used in residential treatment programs, accompanying family programs are also frequently delivered in a group format.

Typically, families of inpatient substance abuse clients are invited to the treatment facility when the client has completed approximately 75% of the inpatient stay. Families are often brought to the campus or treatment facility and offered housing for several days while they complete the family program. During their stay, families will have individual family meetings in which they work with the substance-abusing member and a counselor. In addition, they are typically provided with group counseling that includes members of other families who have a substance-abusing member. Groups are usually offered to parents, adult partners, and children, and are specifically designed to focus on the needs of the particular group.

Counseling groups for family members of individuals with an SUD are not the same as support groups (which are discussed below) available to the same population. In the case of group counseling, a trained facilitator will provide leadership, direction, and support throughout the group process. For this reason, counselors providing this form of treatment need to be trained in substance abuse counseling, the impact of substance abuse on a family, and the principles and techniques associated with group counseling. The group facilitator is responsible for simultaneously noting the whole of the group experience—the overt group content and the covert group dynamics. Participation as a group facilitator requires recognizing and experiencing the dynamic processes that continually evolve within the group context. The group facilitator is also responsible for modeling group participation. As a member of the group, the facilitator must remain open and genuine and should model appropriate listening and responding skills. Finally, the group facilitator will be the content expert. In other words, the group facilitator will hold knowledge relevant to the focus of the group, in this case, issues likely to affect families that have a substance-abusing member (Yalom, 2005).

A Model for Working With Families With a Substance-Abusing Member

In their book *The Responsibility Trap: A Blueprint for Treating the Alcoholic Family,* Bepko and Krestan (1985) presented a three-stage model for treating family members of individuals with an SUD. These stages include establishment of boundaries and identity, commitment and stability, and clarification and legacy.

Establishment of Boundaries and Identity

As discussed earlier, families always strive to achieve equilibrium. In doing so, the family establishes a balance that enables functioning to occur. Families will inevitably will find a place of balance, whether functioning is healthy and supports the growth and development of the family and the individual members or unhealthy and unable to support positive growth for the individual family members.

In families with a substance-abusing member, equilibrium is likely to have been developed in response to the substance abuse issue. Therefore, although the family may be balanced, it is not likely to be functional. Bepko and Krestan (1985) argued that the first stage of family counseling with such a family should be aimed at establishing boundaries and identity.

A family is a system composed of a variety of subsystems. Minuchin (2006) argued that a family should be structurally hierarchical and that the resulting subsystems within it should reflect this hierarchy. For example, in a traditional two-parent family, a parental subsystem should exist and hold the top tier within the hierarchy. This boundary should be clear to all family members. Although structural theory requires some flexibility with boundaries, it supports the notion that boundaries need to remain firm and clear (Minuchin, 2006). In the stage of counseling wherein boundaries and identity are established, the focus of therapy should be on the newly configured family (i.e., the family with a member in early recovery as opposed to a member abusing substances) that is likely to be out of equilibrium. This newly configured family will need to establish new boundaries that support the recovery of the individual with an SUD and the growth and healthy development of all of the family members. Equilibrium for such a family has historically existed around the substance abuse issue, and the family is likely to be drawn toward achieving equilibrium using the same behavior patterns that provided balance in the past. It is therefore important that the counselor works to assist the family in tolerating the anxiety associated with disequilibrium and a shift in the boundaries and structure of the family as they work to establish a new foundation for balance that incorporates and supports the new normal for the family.

In this stage, the counselor and the family will identify behavior patterns that are working and those that are not. In addition, the counselor will want to directly address the anxiety within the system. As the family seeks to change, members are likely to feel anxious. This anxiety should be explored and identified, and distinctions should be made between anxiety associated with a real threat and the anxiety associated with the positive changes occurring within the family. Family members should be encouraged to tolerate the anxiety surrounding the changes in the family and resist resorting to old patterns that supported the substance abuse within the system.

An example of the manifestation of anxiety that the counselor will want the family to tolerate might involve the family mascot. The mascot is likely to have taken on the role of making the family laugh in order to distract them from the true impact of the substance-abusing behavior. Perhaps in counseling the family, the counselor notes the discomfort of the family mascot and recognizes the mascot's attempts at continuous humor throughout the counseling process. The counselor may want to gently confront the mascot and assist the mascot in exploring his or her true feelings. This process might involve helping the mascot to consider a new identity within the family that does not exclusively depend on breaking up family tension with humor. Such a change is very likely to create anxiety for the mascot, specifically regarding how he or she will fit in within the newly developing family structure. Mascots' attempts at humor throughout the counseling process are likely to relate to their desire to minimize this anxiety by bringing the family back into equilibrium using old behavior patterns. In working through this, the client can be encouraged to disrupt this behavior and tolerate the accompanying anxiety.

Commitment and Stability

The second stage of counseling described by Bepko and Krestan (1985) is commitment and stability. During this stage, the family continues adjusting to its new structure. Although the family is still focused on the SUD throughout this stage, the focus shifts to hoping that sobriety for the affected family member will stick. In order to facilitate this outcome and promote further healing, the counselor encourages individual family members to openly share their experiences within the family and express unmet needs. This is a time of immense healing, as families move toward a more solidified version of their new state of equilibrium. In addition, it is a time when individual family members are encouraged to express honestly their desires and feelings as the family continues to work toward meeting individual members' needs. This stage represents a time of intense work for the family.

The commitment and stability stage of the counseling process is likely to be painful for the family. Members are encouraged to express candidly their individual experiences of living with a family member who struggles with an SUD. A child might break down recalling and expressing instances of being let down by a substance-abusing parent. Siblings might express rage at their substance-abusing brother or sister and at their parents for ignoring their needs. Or a parent might express the deep pain of not knowing if their child would survive the disorder. These expressions of intense feeling are likely to induce guilt as family members face and struggle with their inability to support each other throughout the active stages of the SUD. It is important that counselors attend to these feelings. These negative feelings can be intense and are likely to produce extreme discomfort. They need to be processed and resolved and remain a focus for the counselor during this stage of treatment in order to protect the family from relapse.

Clarification and Legacy

Finally, the family will enter the clarification and legacy stage of treatment. This is the stage in which families gain stability and balance. Family members are encouraged to engage in new behaviors throughout this stage that promote and support sobriety and the family's newfound structure. This stage is also filled with promise and provides family members with the opportunity for growth and change as roles and rules are renegotiated. As this process occurs, individual family members are sometimes able to rediscover goals and dreams that may have been neglected or pushed aside. As the family becomes more functional and supportive, individual members are increasingly able to rediscover their potential. For example, children who may have adopted the scapegoat role might begin to change their role and identity within the family. Whereas acting out and sabotaging their future may have provided the basis for established behavior patterns in the past, they might reconsider that path and begin to achieve and succeed. As these changes continue to occur and solidify, the family will begin to shift its legacy and support and encourage the growth and potential of the individual members.

In addition to the stage theory proposed, Bepko and Krestan (1985, pp. 81–83) provided 12 questions to guide professional counselors in assessing families, which I have modified below.

1. Where is the addiction in the family?
   Discern who in the family is struggling with an SUD.
2. Who is the most affected by the addiction?
   This is generally a difficult question to answer. In fact, it might be more accurate to discover how the addiction in the family has affected each member, as the impact will vary.
3. Is it really addiction?
   It may be helpful to understand where on the continuum the SUD falls. This information will assist the counselor and the family in predicting the potential course of treatment.
4. In what phase is the drinking/drugging behavior?
   This question is related to the previous question. Understanding

the severity of the SUD can assist the counselor and the family in understanding and anticipating the course of treatment.

5. What phase is the family in?
   The counselor will want to determine whether the family is at the establishment of boundaries and identity stage, at the commitment and stability stage, or at the clarification and legacy stage. This assessment will assist the counselor immensely in determining the optimal course of treatment.

6. What phase of the life cycle is the addict and/or alcoholic in?
   The life stage of the family member with the SUD is pertinent to the impact of the addiction on the family. If the substance-abusing family member is a parent, it will affect the family in different ways than if it is a child in the system. This information will also influence treatment goals for the family.

7. What does the family think about the addiction?
   Understanding how the family perceives the substance abuse is important. In order to effectively treat the family, the counselor needs to meet the members where they are. Families will have varying degrees of knowledge regarding substance abuse disorders. In addition, levels of denial will affect family treatment. Some families will be better able to accept the substance abuse and be more open to treatment than others.

8. What solutions has the family already attempted?
   The counselor will want to explore what forms of treatment and other strategies the family has engaged in already. This information will further ensure that the current treatment fits the family's unique needs.

9. What does the secrecy map look like?
   Virtually every family with a substance-abusing member has established a secrecy map. The rules that evolve to support the SUD within the family inevitably require a level of secrecy. In every family, the manifestation and scope of the secrecy will vary. It is important for the counselor and the family to understand how secrecy and denial have manifested within the family in order to change these patterns and work toward a new structure that promotes honesty.

10. What is the family history of addiction?
    Understanding the family history of addiction provides important information. Substance abuse runs in families, and the patterns that emerge are often multigenerational (Cook, 2007). In order to break these patterns, a clear picture of the familial history of substance abuse will be helpful. A genogram can be used to depict such patterns and can be useful in fully understanding the extent of the legacy of substance abuse within the family.

11. What patterns of over- and underresponsibility exist?
    In dysfunctional family systems, there is a tendency for individu-

als to overfunction or to underfunction, resulting in an imbalance in the assignment of responsibilities (Williams & Jimenez, 2012). Oftentimes in a family with a substance-abusing member, the enabler will be overresponsible as a means of compensating for the substance abuser's inability to consistently meet typical expectations. This situation may be true for the family hero as well. The scapegoat and the substance abuser, on the other hand, may be underfunctioning and irresponsible with regard to activities common in the maintenance of family life. These patterns become ingrained within the family and will not necessarily fade in response to sobriety. The counselor and the family will need to explore this issue and identify where these behavioral changes need to be made. As the family moves toward creating a new structure and balance, the issues of over- and underresponsibility need to be addressed directly.

12. How is the power structure perceived in the family?

As previously mentioned, according to Minuchin (2006), the structure of the family system is of critical importance to family functioning. The structure of a family is healthiest when it is hierarchical, with the adult caretakers within the system assuming the top tier of the hierarchy. It is not uncommon in families with a substance-abusing member to see a shift in power within the system, such that the adult caretakers may not occupy the top level within the hierarchy. When a caretaker is struggling with an SUD, that person's ability to hold and effectively use power diminishes. This situation may lead another family member (oftentimes the family hero) to occupy an adult role. In this case, a child often assumes a position of power in order to maintain equilibrium and keep the family functioning, which can result in the parentification of that child (Hedges, 2012). In treatment, the counselor will want to address any power imbalances or instances of role confusion within the family, as these are likely to have become a vehicle for maintaining equilibrium that has become entrenched within the family.

Motivational Interviewing (MI)

One of the popular techniques used in the treatment of individuals with an SUD is motivational interviewing (MI). Originally described by Miller (1983), MI began as a means of working with "problem drinkers." Miller and Rollnick (2013) subsequently detailed the development of a comprehensive treatment technique outlined in their book *Motivational Interviewing: Helping People Change*, currently in its third edition. As suggested by the title, MI is a technique centered on helping individuals identify and increase their level of motivation to change. The counseling involves a process whereby the counselor engages in a person-centered conversation with the client that is intended to strengthen that client's motivation and commitment to change.

MI is described as a collaborative process in which the counselor and the client participate as equal partners in assisting the client in changing a behavior. Using preexisting knowledge regarding how people might effectively assist others, MI evolved as a method for guiding people through the process of behavioral change.

One of the initial objectives of MI is to assist individuals in examining their behavior in the context of their personal values and goals, assuming that change is most likely to occur when behavior is linked to these factors. Because a primary focus of MI is to increase an individual's intrinsic motivation to change, one method used in MI is to tie the client's behaviors to values and consequences that are most important him or her. MI was initially used with substance-abusing clients and focused on changing behaviors associated with abusing drugs and alcohol. Thus, the use of MI in the treatment of clients who live with a substance-abusing family member seems a logical application of these techniques, as these clients, like those with an SUD, are likely to indicate behavioral change as a goal of counseling.

A basic premise underlying MI is that change is difficult and requires a readiness that cannot be assumed. Although we might assume that all clients are in counseling in order to facilitate a change of some sort, this may, in fact, not be the case. Clients may want changes to occur in their lives but may be at very different points regarding their genuine commitment to participate in the steps necessary to actualize the desired change. Therefore, an initial focus in MI is to evaluate the client's readiness to change. The underlying assumption for engaging in this process is that individuals who are not ready will not change. Understanding how ready an individual client is to make changes provides a baseline for beginning the counseling process.

The Stages of Change

MI has adopted Prochaska, DiClemente, and Norcross's (2003) Stages of Change Model as a means of assessing a client's readiness for change. This model provides five levels of readiness for change and is used to assist the counselor and the client in understanding where the counseling process should begin. Specific strategies and techniques for moving the client along the change continuum have been identified and can be applied once there is an awareness of where along this continuum a client is regarding the identified change.

The identified stages include the following:

- *Precontemplation.* The client is currently not considering a change. Changing is outside of awareness for the client.
- *Contemplation.* The client sees the possibility for change but is ambivalent and unsure of how to begin the process.

- *Determination.* The client has decided that he or she wants to change and is willing to commit to change but has not yet formulated a plan. The client is unsure of what to do.
- *Action.* The client has taken action steps toward making the desired change but is unstable in the process. The client is "doing" things to change but may not feel differently.
- *Maintenance.* The client has achieved the articulated goals and has made the change. The focus is now on maintaining the change.

Another assumption in MI is that individuals are virtually always ambivalent about change. Practitioners using MI view a lack of motivation as unresolved ambivalence. Intertwined with the notion of ambivalence is the construct of motivation. MI practitioners see motivation as a necessary element of change. It is assumed that talking through ambivalence and identifying its source leads one to internalize the motivation to change. Working with ambivalence tends to increase motivation and move clients further along on the model-of-change continuum.

Strategies and Techniques

MI offers a number of strategies and techniques used to facilitate the working through of ambivalence and movement toward increased motivation (Sobell & Sobell, 2008). Many of these strategies are quite familiar to professional counselors, whereas other might be less well-known. The techniques are evidence-based and can be used regardless of where the client is along the stages-of-change continuum.

Asking Permission

Asking permission involves inviting the client to discuss difficult issues or behaviors that are interfering with his or her quality of life. The premise for using this strategy is the assumption that people will respond more favorably to this approach than to being lectured or heavily directed. When a counselor is dealing with a family member of an individual with an SUD, this assumption is very important. As has already been established, this population of clients has a tendency to shut down, making the relationship-building aspect of the therapeutic process vital.

Examples of asking permission with this client population might include the use of questions such as the following: "Do you mind if we discuss your family history related to addiction and substance abuse?" or "I notice from your history that you have struggled with anxiety. Would you mind if we go back and discuss the sources of this anxiety?"

Change Talk

Change talk involves helping clients articulate their own motivations for changing. The premise for using this technique is that when individuals are able to articulate their desire and reasons to change, better outcomes are more likely. There are several techniques that a counselor can use in order to elicit change talk from a client. One is pointing out discrepancies. In this case, the therapist points out to the client a discrepancy between what the client is saying he or she wants and a behavior that might be antithetical to the change occurring.

For example, a parent of a substance-abusing child might state, "I just want my son/daughter to understand the consequences of his/her continued drug use." At the same time, this parent may be covering for the child with school officials or other parents, allowing the child privileges such as using the family car, giving the child an allowance for minimal contributions to the family, offering tremendous assistance with homework, and so forth. The counselor might want to point out this particular discrepancy by stating, "You seem to want very much for your child to understand the link between his/her behavior and the consequences that he/she might face. At the same time, it seems like it is very difficult for you to allow some of the natural consequences to occur for your child."

Eliciting change talk can be relatively easy or extremely difficult, depending on which stage the client is in regarding his or her readiness for change. For clients in the determination, action, or maintenance stages, evoking change talk generally requires little effort on the part of the counselor. On the other hand, for clients in the precontemplation or contemplation stages, engaging the client in change talk can require significant effort. Clients in the precontemplation stage are not committed to change and may not be making the connection between their current behavior and the likelihood that they will reach desired goals. One suggestion for assisting clients in engaging in change talk in the contemplation stage would be to ask them to envision their future if they do not make any changes and compare that to what things might look like if they are able to change.

Often a client who has a family member struggling with an SUD will insist that the substance abuser change. The family member may begin the therapeutic process with the goal of learning what he or she can do to change the substance abuser; hence, the family member has not yet considered that he or she might need to change. Suggestions for working with such clients at this stage in the process might include asking clients to describe their level of success in changing the individual with the SUD. In addition, the counselor might ask clients, "What are some changes that you could make that do not involve the substance abuser but might help you to increase your overall well-being?" or "What do you think might happen if you don't change anything at all about how you cope with and respond to substance-abusing family member?"

The thing to keep in mind with these techniques is that within the context of MI, they are being used to elicit change talk, not necessarily to evoke the change itself. The goal of this technique in MI, as opposed to similar techniques in other treatment frameworks, is to get the client to engage in talk that specifically articulates change—how they might change, what different changes might look like, what the future holds if they do not change, and so forth.

Exploring Importance and Confidence

Exploring importance and confidence is used to assess the value (importance) the client genuinely attributes to the targeted change and the client's sense of his or her ability to actually make that change (confidence). Understanding the importance a client attributes to making the identified change assists the counselor in assessing the client's readiness to change, speaks directly to the client's motivation, and may assist the counselor and client in working through ambivalence.

One of the evidence-based techniques used to explore importance and confidence is the Readiness for Change Ruler (Hesse, 2006). This tool can be used to assess the level of importance a client has ascribed to a specific change as well as the level of confidence the client feels regarding his or her ability to make the change. Using a scale ranging from 1 (*not at all*) through 10 (*100%*), the counselor can ask the client the following questions: "How important is it to you to make this change?" "How confident are you that you can make this change?" and "How ready are you to make this change?" This tool can be applied throughout the counseling process to assess progress in the client's readiness to change over time. This simple tool can provide a concrete indication of where a client is in terms of his or her readiness for change, which can assist both the client and the counselor in determining what might effectively support the client in moving up the ruler to a higher level of readiness.

Open-Ended Questions

Every professional counselor has been taught the meaning and use of open-ended questions. Using an open-ended question, we elicit discussion rather than a simple answer. Asking the client how he or she felt about something may elicit a simple "good" or "bad," but it also allows the client to use his or her own words to articulate an experience with a richer explanation of what the experience was like. In addition to opening up the conversation, open-ended questions allow the counselor to display and use empathy, another skill very familiar to the professional counselor. The importance of a counselor's ability to feel and show genuine empathy cannot be overstated, as this kind of connection is what allows for trust. As established earlier, trust may be a significant issue for family members of individuals struggling with an SUD, making the use of empathy and any other trust-building techniques extremely important in working with this population.

Reflective Listening

The art and skills associated with reflective listening are also very familiar to professional counselors. They are another means of establishing a relationship whereby the client feels heard and understood. Reflecting back to the client what the counselor has heard is deceptively powerful and allows the counselor to then explore the experience on a deeper level. This technique provides another mechanism for building trust and learning more about the client's readiness to change.

Normalizing

Normalizing is used to communicate to clients that having difficulty changing is not an uncommon experience. The idea is that the counselor can offer clients the assurance that they are not alone in experiencing difficulty in attempting to make a change. Oftentimes, clients who are struggling with an addiction themselves or who have a family member with an SUD feel isolated and lonely. They may feel that the kinds of changes they are required to make in order to live a more meaningful and healthy life are impossible. Using normalizing, a counselor can help clients to understand that although changing in this manner is difficult, it is not impossible and they are not alone in their experience.

Decisional Balancing

Although decisional balancing can be used anytime throughout treatment, it is particularly helpful in assisting clients in understanding ambivalence and how this affects their readiness for change. With decisional balancing, clients are asked to articulate (or write down) reasons to change a behavior, anticipating possible good outcomes if they change. Next they do the same exercise but articulate reasons not to change the behavior. This process allow for an in-depth look at how the particular behavior is maintained for that client. This exercise is also referred to as the Payoff Matrix (Hazeldon Betty Ford Foundation, n.d.-b.)

Let's look at decisional balancing in practice. Your client, Lakshmi, is continuing to enable her alcoholic husband. She regularly makes excuses for him. She walks on eggshells and works hard to keep things at home "perfect," and she has isolated herself from her own support system. Even though she and her husband are both employed full time outside of the home, she takes care of virtually everything regarding the house, including cooking, cleaning, grocery shopping, managing the finances, and yard work. Lakshmi has acknowledged that she needs to make some changes but does not know how to begin this process. She is the child of an alcoholic mother and grew up in a home where she assumed virtually the same role she has in her current family. She would like to start by attempting to rebuild a support system. When asked to complete a decisional balance exercise looking at this particular change, this is what she revealed (see Table 9).

Table 9
Decisional Balancing

Positive Outcomes	Negative Outcomes
Positives about remaining isolated	Negatives about remaining isolated
It is familiar and in a strange way it feels safe sometimes.	I am often lonely and scared; it is not good for my children.
Positives about changing	Negatives about changing
It would feel good to open up to someone; I could have friends and engage in activities I enjoy.	I would have to be honest with others, and I will feel like a failure; people might judge me and I will feel ashamed and be isolated.

Using this chart, the counselor and the client can begin to explore Lakshmi's ambivalence. This information reveals some of the sources of that ambivalence; thus, those issues can be explored at a deeper level.

The Columbo Approach

The Columbo approach, named after a popular television character who engaged regularly in simply stating observations, involves noting circumstances, discrepancies, and statements without judging or blaming. Using this approach, the counselor might point out a discrepancy in a matter-of-fact manner and indicate a curiosity and desire to understand how that discrepancy might make sense in the mind of the client. In posing such discrepancies in such a manner, the counselor is attempting to avoid a defensive response that is likely to result in the client shutting down and resisting the opportunity to explore a potential roadblock to change.

An example might be the counselor stating, "I am confused. I have noticed that on the one hand you say that you are very sick of being the family caretaker, and, at the same time, you continue to take on additional responsibilities that might be more appropriately taken on by other family members." In this example, the counselor would remain completely nonjudgmental and pose the observation out of genuine curiosity.

Statements Supporting Self-Efficacy

Self-efficacy, defined by Bandura, Caprara, Barbaranelli, Gerbino, and Pastorelli (2003) as a person's belief in his or her ability to change in specific situations, is essential to succeeding in any endeavor involving a major life change. This issue was mentioned tangentially during the discussion about the client's perception of the importance of a particular change and the client's confidence in his or her ability to make the change. However, here I am talking about a strategy for helping to increase the self-efficacy a client experiences. For example, you, the counselor, might point out the changes that you have seen the client make, perhaps the smaller changes that are laying the groundwork for achieving a primary goal. Sometimes, when individuals are attempting to make a change in their life that they perceive as monumental, the small changes they make along the way can get lost, as they continue to focus on the primary outcome they are seeking. In this case, it is important to acknowledge the incremental changes for clients in the hopes that they can internalize that information and increase their level of self-efficacy.

Applying MI to working with families with a substance-abusing member may provide a structure that allows these clients to learn about the change process as it relates to both themselves and to the substance abuser in their life. The model described can provide a rich understanding of issues like denial, control, and shame. In addition, the techniques provide a means of engaging these clients in nonthreatening conversation that might provide illumination and a focus for moving forward in their own lives, even if the individual with the SUD does not make significant changes.

Family Behavior Loop Mapping

Family Behavior Loop Mapping (FBLM) is a family systems technique for treating the entire addictive family (Leipman, Flachier, & Tareen, 2012). As the name suggests, this technique involves mapping family interactions. To be specific, a detailed analysis of every family member's thoughts, feelings, and behavior is conducted and then mapped via a flow diagram that both the clinician and the family can study. In conducting this analysis, the counselor will seek to understand on a step-by-step basis the precise thoughts of every family member during times of substance use and abuse and during times of abstinence. In this way, a clear picture begins to develop that highlights the differences between times of active use and times of abstinence.

One interesting finding is that this activity will also serve to highlight aspects of functioning that are, in fact, healthier during times of abstinence. It is important to note though, that in studies conducted to test the use of FBLM with couples, researchers found that on a scale measuring a variety of areas of functioning, for 17 of the 20 couples under study, at least one dimension of functioning decreased during abstinence (Leipman, Nirenberg, Doolittle, Broffman, & Sylvia, 1993). This finding suggested that the substance use, although unhealthy, actually did serve an important function for the family. In creating the flow chart, both the counselor and the client are able to see this information and consciously process the ways in which the addiction might serve to preserve homeostasis for the family.

After the map is completed, previously unacknowledged incentives for using and for relapse should be revealed. This revelation allows the client and the counselor to begin to create a corrective map. During this process, the counselor and client work together to identify any advantages gained by using. Once these have been identified, a plan for achieving the same advantages during abstinence is developed. After the advantage is identified and moved to times of abstinence, the family practices the new behaviors by enacting them and processing these activities.

One of the most significant and important phases in FBLM process involves the family interviews, during which the counselor and the clients seek to understand precisely what occurs within the family. Using flip charts, dry erase boards, sticky notes, or any other means of mapping, the counselor will attempt to draw what the clients report. This process is done using three different symbols: one to indicate thoughts, one to indicate feelings, and one to indicate behaviors. Most often a rectangle, an oval, and a diamond are used, each designated with a different aspect of functioning within the family. Arrows are then used to connect different processes as they are presented.

One of the goals of this process is to discover patterns, looking to see what behaviors, thoughts, and feelings lead to others. In some cases, these patterns will appear in the form of loops whereby there is a cyclical nature to the interactions that is predictable within the family. Oftentimes there will be several loops. Uncovering predictable patterns in families allows the counselor and the client to precisely identify how the patterns are maintained. Through the mapping process, one piece of information that is likely to emerge is the identification of the roles that specific family members play. In addition, feelings of guilt, shame, or anger might be identified at particular points within the loops. Dysfunctional behavior might be identified as occurring at specific points within the identified cycles. Revelation of these patterns makes it is easier for family members to consider where in the process changes might be most beneficial. In addition, the thoughts, feelings, and behaviors of family members during times of abstinence are revealed, providing information that might be applied to times of use and abuse Finally, this process allows for the development of targeted strategies for changing the dysfunctional patterns that are occurring in fairly predictable ways.

Al-Anon, Co-Dependents Anonymous, and National Association for Children of Alcoholics Groups

In addition to treatment strategies that exist for clinicians, several self-help groups have become popular and are often thought to be helpful as supplemental supports for families struggling with addiction. Probably the most popular of these is Al-Anon (see their website at http://www.al-anon.org). Al-Anon is a group based on the widely embraced 12-step model for drug abusers and alcoholics (see below). Originally begun by Lois W., the wife of Bill W., Al-Anon was structured to provide support for spouses of substance abusers. Over time, however, Al-Anon expanded and is now available to anyone in a close relationship with a substance abuser. In fact, there are now specialized Al-Anon groups (e.g., parents of substance-abusing children) that seek to provide more focused support for particular groups whose needs and experiences may be unique.

Al-Anon is a recovery program for individuals affected by addiction and is delivered and run by individuals in recovery. Al-Anon provides a structured framework for working on issues often associated with living with a substance-abusing family member. Working on the premise that living with an individual who has an SUD promotes feelings, thoughts, and behaviors that limit an individual's functioning, Al-Anon seeks to provide a supportive environment and a program that can be used to promote healthier relationships and an increased sense of well-being.

Three other groups very similar to Al-Anon are Alateen (Al-Anon Family Groups, n.d.), Co-Dependents Anonymous (CoDA; see their website at http://www.coda.org), and the National Association for Children of Alcoholics (NACOA; see their website at http://www.nacoa.org). Applying the same principles and format as Al-Anon, each of these groups seeks to meet the needs of a specific population of individuals affected by addiction. Alateen, for example, is structured to meet the needs of adolescents who are affected by addiction or alcoholism. CoDA serves individuals who identify as codependent, and NACOA is structured to meet the needs of adult individuals who were raised by a caregiver struggling with an SUD.

All of these groups are based on the 12-steps of AA:

1. We admitted we were powerless over alcohol—that our lives had become unmanageable.
2. Came to believe that a Power greater than ourselves could restore us to sanity.
3. Made a decision to turn our will and our lives over to the care of God *as we understood Him.*
4. Made a searching and fearless moral inventory of ourselves.
5. Admitted to God, to ourselves, and to another human being the exact nature of our wrongs.
6. Were entirely ready to have God remove all these defects of character.
7. Humbly asked Him to remove our shortcomings.
8. Made a list of all persons we had harmed, and became willing to make amends to them all.
9. Made direct amends to such people wherever possible, except when to do so would injure them or others.
10. Continued to take personal inventory and when we were wrong promptly admitted it.

11. Sought through prayer and meditation to improve our conscious contact with God *as we understood Him*, praying only for knowledge of His will for us and the power to carry that out.
12. Having had a spiritual awakening as the result of these steps, we tried to carry this message to alcoholics and to practice these principles in all our affairs.

Note. The Twelve Steps are reprinted with permission of Alcoholics Anonymous World Services, Inc. ("AAWS"). Permission to reprint the Twelve Steps does not mean that AAWS has reviewed or approved the contents of this publication, or that AAWS necessarily agrees with the views expressed herein. A.A. is a program of recovery from alcoholism only—use of the Twelve Steps in connection with programs and activities which are patterned after A.A., but which address other problems, or in any other non-A.A. context, does not imply otherwise.

Case Example for Treatment

Krystal, 45, has just completed her third week of a 28-day residential treatment program for her addiction to alcohol and prescription drugs. She has entered the "family" phase of her program. Her husband, James (age 57), and three of their children are at the treatment center to participate in family counseling.

Krystal and James have been married for 8 years. This is a second marriage for both of them, and between them they have four children: Ryan, 18, James's son from his first marriage who is at college and therefore unable to participate in the family program; Seth, 16, James's second son from his first marriage; Marissa, 11, Krystal's daughter from her first marriage; and Tyler, 6, the biological child of Krystal and James. James's first wife is deceased, and all four children live full time with Krystal and James.

Krystal has been an alcoholic for as long as she can remember. She started drinking in middle school and very quickly knew that she had an SUD, although she did not identify it as such at that stage in her life. Even though she continued to drink heavily, Krystal managed to get through college and begin her adult life. However, it did not take long for her life to spiral out of control. Krystal entered a residential treatment program when she was 25, and sobriety stuck for many years. In fact, Krystal was sober throughout her first marriage and remained very active in her local recovery community. That marriage ended amicably, and Krystal met James one year later.

Krystal and James married within 6 months of meeting each other and began their life together. Blending the two families was a challenge, and Krystal was left with the bulk of dealing with the issues related to this transition. James had a very demanding job and traveled a great deal while Krystal stayed home and managed the household and the children. Within several months of being married, Krystal became pregnant with Tyler. She endured a difficult pregnancy and delivered Tyler by Cesarean section. As a result, Krystal was prescribed narcotic painkillers. Although she did think briefly about refusing them, she decided that she needed them and that she would be fine. However, she very quickly became addicted and began to abuse the medication. Eventually, she began to drink again and began resorting to illegal ways of obtaining prescription medication.

Krystal managed to keep her relapse a secret for several months. However, James began to suspect that something was wrong and confronted her. She denied his accusations and claimed that she was simply tired from her surgery and caring for four children. At the same time, Seth became suspicious and found some pills and empty liquor bottles. Krystal pleaded with him not to tell James or anyone else. She promised to get back into AA and stop using immediately. Seth agreed to keep her secret.

James's work schedule continued to keep him very busy and away from home on a regular basis. Eventually, Marissa became very concerned. She was confused about why her mother was "sick" all of the time. When she finally went to James with her concerns and confusion, he assured her that Krystal was just tired with the baby and would be fine.

The family established a routine and norms that included accommodating Krystal's SUD. Communication was difficult, relationships were strained, and the individual family members found separate ways of dealing with the stress. Ryan was caught up in school and in sports, attempting to ensure his acceptance into a college that was far from home. Seth began partying and staying away from home as much as possible. Marissa began to exhibit signs of anxiety and depression that were not picked up by Krystal or James, and Tyler became clingy and was having difficulties getting along with other children. Despite all of these dysfunctional patterns, nobody talked about the substance abuse issue within the family.

Finally, one afternoon, Seth returned home to find Krystal passed out on the kitchen floor. He immediately called 911, and she was rushed to the hospital. Her stomach was pumped and she was admitted to the psychiatric unit where she would undergo detoxification. From here, Krystal was admitted to the 28-day treatment program she was currently attending. She has attended groups and individual therapy sessions, and she has gotten reconnected with the 12-step recovery program. Krystal will now begin the treatment phase during which she will work with her family.

Discussion

Use the case of Krystal and apply the various treatment models and strategies described in this chapter.

CONCLUSION

Working with any population of clients requires an understanding of the potential issues and challenges faced by that group. The material covered in this book is meant to prepare the professional counselor for working with family members of individuals with an SUD. Substance use and abuse affect the entire family. Therefore, it is important to have an understanding of family dynamics and theories and a working knowledge of how these might apply to individual cases. This knowledge includes familiarity with both the larger frameworks for understanding families (i.e., the concepts of equilibrium and homeostasis and the primary theories used to frame work with families) as well as the specific characteristics common for families with a substance-abusing member. In addition, the professional counselor must consider the developmental implications of living in a family with a substance-abusing member and apply developmental theory to specific cases.

Once the theoretical groundwork is laid, counselors can consider the specific ways in which this population has been characterized and conceptualized. Understanding the construct of codependency provides one means of characterizing the population of individuals who have lived with a substance-abusing family member. And understanding the variety of issues linked to familial SUD provides a basis for assessing a client's individual experience.

Finally, consideration of the client's cultural contexts, both in general and regarding substance use and abuse, is critical. Understanding the nature and perception of substance use and abuse from the client's cultural or lifestyle viewpoint is essential in gaining a clear picture of the issues discussed. This information is also vital in determining the most appropriate treatment option for each client.

Overall, it is my hope that this book has provided the beginning counselor with a tool. It has been my intention to create a book that synthesizes what we currently know about individuals who live with substance-abusing family members and apply it to our identity as professional counselors. It has been an honor and a pleasure to share this information with you!

REFERENCES

Abbott, P., & Chase, D. M. (2008). Culture and substance abuse: Impact of culture affects approach to treatment. *Psychiatric Times, 1,* 43–46.

Abdel-Mawgoud, M., Fateem, L., & Al-Sharif, A. I. (1995). Development of a comprehensive treatment program for chemical dependency at Al Amal Hospital, Dammam. *Journal of Substance Abuse Treatment, 12,* 369–376.

Adkinson, S. E., Grohman, K., Colder, C. R., Leonard, K., Orrange-Torchia, T., Peterson, E., & Eiden, R. E. (2013). Impact of fathers' alcohol problems on the development of effortful control in early adolescence. *Journal of Studies on Alcohol and Drugs, 74,* 674–683.

Agrawal, A., & Lynskey, M. Y. (2014). Genetics of substance use disorders. In S. H. Rhee & A. Ronald (Eds.), *Behavior genetics of psychopathology* (pp. 185–230). New York, NY: Springer Science and Business Media.

Agrawal, A., Narayanan, G., & Oltmanns, T. F. (2013). Personality pathology and alcohol dependence at midlife in a community setting. *Personality Disorders: Theory, Research, and Treatment, 4,* 55–61. doi:10.1037/a0030224

Al-Anon Family Groups. (n.d.). *How will Alateen help me?* Retrieved from http://al-anon.alateen.org/for-alateen

Ambruster, E. W. (2008). Attachment and bonding: Correlations between relationship and anxiety among adult college students. *Dissertation Abstracts International: Section B. The Sciences and Engineering, 69*(6-B).

American Counseling Association. (2009). *The ACA encyclopedia of counseling.* Alexandria, VA: Author.

American Psychiatric Association. (2000). *Diagnostic and statistical manual of mental disorders* (4th ed., text rev.). Washington, DC: Author.

American Psychiatric Association. (2013). *Diagnostic and statistical manual of mental disorders* (5th ed.). Arlington, VA: Author.

American Society of Addiction Medicine. (n.d.). *Definition of addiction.* Retrieved from http://www.asam.org/for-the-public/definition-of-addiction

Anderson, K. F. (2013). Diagnosing discrimination: Stress from perceived racism and the mental and physical health effects. *Sociological Inquiry, 83,* 55–81.

Arnold, C., & Fisch, R. (2011). *The impact of complex trauma on development.* Lanham, MD: Jason Aronson.

Backer-Fulghum, L. M., Patock-Peckham, J. A., King, K. M., Toufa, L., & Hagen, L. (2012). The stress-response dampening hypothesis: How self-esteem and stress act as mechanisms between negative parental bonds and alcohol-related problems in emerging adulthood. *Addictive Behaviors, 37,* 477–484.

Bailey, K. M., & Stewart, S. H. (2014). Relations among trauma, PTSD, and substance misuse: The scope of the problem. In P. Ouimette & J. P. Read (Eds.), *Trauma and substance abuse: Causes, consequences, and treatment of comorbid disorders* (2nd ed., pp. 11–34). Washington, DC: American Psychological Association.

Bandura, A., Caprara, G. V., Barbaranelli, C., Gerbino, M., & Pastorelli, C. (2003). Role of affective self-regulatory efficacy in diverse spheres of psychosocial functioning. *Child Development, 74,* 769–782.

Beck, A. T. (1976). *Cognitive therapy and emotional disorders.* New York, NY: Universities International Press.

Belles, S., Budde, A., Moesgen, D., & Klein, M. (2011). Parental problem drinking predicts implicit alcohol expectancy in adolescents and young adults. *Addictive Behaviors, 36,* 1091–1094.

Bepko, C., & Krestan, J. A. (1985). *The responsibility trap: A blueprint for treating the alcoholic family.* New York, NY: Simon & Schuster.

Best, D. W., Wilson, A. S., MacLean, S., Savic, M., Reed, M., Bruun, A., & Lubman, D. I. (2014). Patterns of family conflict and their impact on substance use and psychological outcomes in a sample of young people in treatment. *Vulnerable Children and Youth Studies, 9,* 114–122.

Black, C. (2001). *It will never happen to me.* Bainbridge Island, WA: MAC.

Blier, P. (2013). Neurotransmitter targeting in the treatment of depression. *Journal of Clinical Psychiatry, 74,* 19–24.

Blum, H. (2013). Dissociation and its disorders. *Psychoanalytic Inquiry, 33,* 427–438.

Bowen, M. (1978). *Family therapy in clinical practice*. Lanham, MD: Rowan and Littlefield.

Bowlby, R. (2004). *Fifty years of attachment theory*. London, England: Karnac Books.

Broderick, P. C., & Blewitt, P. (2014). *The life span: Human development for helping professionals* (4th ed.). New York, NY: Pearson.

Brooks, F., & McHenry, B. (2015). *A contemporary approach to substance use disorders and addiction counseling* (2nd ed.) Alexandria, VA: American Counseling Association.

Brown, L. M. (1981). Substance abuse and America: Historical perspective on the federal response to a social phenomenon. *Journal of the National Medical Association, 73*, 497–506.

Buckholdt, K. E., Perra, G. R., & Jobe-Shields, L. (2014). Intergenerational transmission of emotional dysregulation through parental invalidation of emotions: Implications for adolescent internalizing and externalizing behaviors. *Journal of Child and Family Studies, 23*, 324–332.

Calderwood, K. A., & Rajesparam, A. (2014). A critique of the codependency concept considering the best interests of the child. *Families in Society, 95*, 171–178.

Caron Foundation. (n.d.). *Family engagement*. Retrieved from http://www.caron.org/proven-treatment/family-engagement

Carroll, K. M., Sholomskas, D., Syracuse, G., Ball, S. A., Nuro, K., & Fenton, L. R. (2005). We don't train in vain: A dissemination trial of three strategies of training clinicians in cognitive–behavioral therapy. *Journal of Consulting and Clinical Psychology, 73*, 106–115.

Castro, F., & Alarcon, E. (2002). Integrating cultural variables into drug abuse prevention and treatment with racial/ethnic minorities. *Journal of Drug Issues, 32*, 783–810.

Catherall, D. R. (2004). *Handbook of stress, trauma, and the family*. Hoboken, NJ: Taylor & Francis.

Celani, D. P. (2005). *Leaving home: The art of separating from your difficult family*. New York, NY: Columbia University Press.

Cermak, T. L. (1986). Diagnostic criteria for codependency. *Journal of Psychoactive Drugs, 18*, 15–20.

Cermak, T. L. (1991). Co-addiction as a disease. *Psychiatric Annals, 21*, 266–272.

Chan, P. T., Doan, S. N., & Tompson, M. C. (2014). Stress generation in a developmental context: The role of youth depressive symptoms, maternal depression, the parent–child relationship, and family stress. *Journal of Family Psychology, 28*, 32–41.

Chaney, M. P., & Brubaker, M. D. (2012). Addiction in LGBTQ communities: Influences, treatment, and prevention. *Journal of LGBT Issues in Counseling, 6*, 234–236.

Cheng, A. W., Lee, C. S., & Iwamoto, D. K. (2012). Heavy drinking, poor mental health, and substance use among Asian-Americans in the NLAAS: A gender-based comparison. *Asian-American Journal of Psychology, 3,* 160–167.

Cicero, T. J., Ellis, M. S., Surratt, H. L., & Kurtz, S. P. (2014). The changing face of heroin use in the United States: A retrospective analysis of the past 50 years. *JAMA Psychiatry, 71,* 821–826.

Cochran, B. N., & Cauce, A. M. (2006). Characteristics of lesbian, gay, bisexual, and transgender individuals entering substance abuse treatment. *Journal of Substance Abuse Treatment, 30,* 135–146.

Cohen-Filipic, K. C. (2014). Guilt, blame and responsibility: The experiences of parents and clinicians providing services to adolescents with co-occurring mental health and substance abuse challenges. *Dissertation Abstracts International: Section A. Humanities and Social Sciences, 74*(9-A)(E).

Cook, L. (2007). Perceived conflict, sibling position, cut-off, and multigenerational transmission in the family of origin of chemically dependent persons: An application of Bowen family systems theory. *Journal of Addictions Nursing, 18,* 130–140.

Cooper, A. M. (1998). Further developments in the clinical diagnosis of narcissistic personality disorder. In E. F. Ronningstam (Ed.), *Disorders of narcissism: Diagnostic, clinical and empirical implications* (pp. 53–74). Arlington, VA: American Psychiatric Association.

Corey, G. (2013). *Theory and practice of counseling and psychotherapy* (9th ed.). Belmont, CA: Cengage.

Crawford, N. D., Borrell, L. N., Galea, S., Ford, C., Latkin, C., & Fuller, C. M. (2013). The influence of neighborhood characteristics on the relationship between discrimination and increased drug-using social ties among illicit drug users. *Journal of Community Health, 38,* 328–337.

Dattilio, F. M. (2010). *Cognitive–behavior therapies with couples and families: A comprehensive guide for clinicians.* New York, NY: Guilford Press.

Dear, G. E., Roberts, C. M., & Lange, L. (2004). Defining codependency: A thematic analysis of published definitions. In S. P. Shohov (Ed.), *Advances in psychology research* (pp. 189–205). Hauppauge, NY: Nova Science.

Denial. (n.d.). In *Merriam Webster dictionary online.* Retrieved from http://www.merriam-webster.com/dictionary/denial

Devine, B. R. (2013). Students with parents involved in substance use or dependence. In E. Rosen & R. Hill (Eds.), *Supporting and educating traumatized students: A guide for school-based professionals* (pp. 119–128). New York, NY: Oxford University Press.

DeVito, E. E., Babuscio, T. A., Nich, C., Ball, S. A., & Carroll, K. M. (2014). Gender differences in clinical outcomes for cocaine dependence: Randomized clinical trials of behavioral therapy and disulfiram. *Drug and Alcohol Dependence, 145,* 156–167.

Dixon-Gordon, K. L., Turner, B. J., & Chapman, A. L. (2011). Psychotherapy for personality disorders. *International Review of Psychiatry, 23,* 282–302.

Donovan, M., & Marlatt, G. A. (2005). *Assessment of addictive behaviors* (2nd ed.). New York, NY: Guilford Press.

Douglass, M. D. (2010). Codependency: Relationship to self and other. *Dissertation Abstracts International: Section B. The Sciences and Engineering, 70*(9-B), 5815.

Drabble, L., Trocki, K. F., Hughes, T. L., Korcha, R. A., & Lown, A. E. (2013). Sexual orientation differences in the relationship between victimization and hazardous drinking among women in the National Alcohol Survey. *Psychology of Addictive Behaviors, 27,* 639–648.

Dunn, M. G., Tarter, R. E., Mezzich, A. C., Vanyukov, M., Kirisci, L., & Kirillova, G. (2002). Origins and consequences of child neglect in substance abuse families. *Clinical Psychology Review, 22,* 1063–1090.

Durst, R., & Lotan, C. (2011). The potential for clinical use of cannabinoids in treatment of cardiovascular disease. *Cardiovascular Therapeutics, 29,* 17–22.

Dwairy, M. A. (2006). *Counseling and psychotherapy with Arabs and Muslims: A culturally sensitive approach.* New York, NY: Teachers College Press.

Edwards, J. (2008). Early splitting and projective identification. *Infant Observation, 11,* 57–65.

Eiden, R. D., Edwards, E. P., & Leonard, K. E. (2007). A conceptual model for the development of externalizing behavior problems among kindergarten children of alcoholic families: Role of parenting and children's self-regulation. *Developmental Psychology, 43,* 1187–1201.

Eitle, T. M., & Eitle, D. (2014). Race, coping strategies, and substance use behaviors: A preliminary analysis examining White and American Indian adolescents. *Substance Use and Misuse, 49,* 315–325.

Ellis, A. (1994). *Reason and emotion in psychotherapy* (Rev. ed.). New York, NY: Kennsington.

Engel, G. L. (1977). The need for a new medical model: A challenge for biomedicine. *Science, 196,* 129–136.

Equilibrium. (n.d.). In *Merriam Webster dictionary online.* Retrieved from http://www.merriam-webster.com/dictionary/equilibrium

Erikson, E. (1950). *Childhood and society.* New York, NY: W. W. Norton.

Erol, R. Y., & Orth, U. (2014). Development of self-esteem and relationship satisfaction in couples: Two longitudinal studies. *Developmental Psychology, 50,* 2291–2303.

Ersche, K. D., Jones, P. S., Williams, G. B., Turton, A. J., Robbins, T. W., & Bullmore, E. T. (2012). Abnormal brain structure implicated in stimulant drug addiction. *Science, 335,* 601–604.

Evens, F. B., III. (2006). *Harry Stack Sullivan: Interpersonal theory and psychotherapy.* Hoboken, NJ: Taylor & Francis.

Fawcett, M. L. (2012). *Experiential approach for developing multicultural counseling competence.* Thousand Oaks, CA: Sage.

Fernando, S. C., Beblo, T., Schlosser, N., Terfehr, K., Otte, C., Löwe, B., . . . Wingenfeld, K. (2014). The impact of self-reported childhood trauma on emotional regulation in borderline personality disorder and major depression. *Journal of Trauma & Dissociation, 15,* 384–401.

Fiorentine, R. (2001). Counseling frequency and the effectiveness of outpatient drug treatment: Revisiting the conclusion that "more is better." *The American Journal of Drug and Alcohol Abuse, 27,* 617–631.

Fish, J. N., Maier, C. A., & Priest, J. B. (2015). Substance abuse treatment response in a Latino family: The role of family conflict. *Journal of Substance Abuse Treatment, 49,* 27–34.

Freud, S. (2010). *Civilization and its discontents.* Mansfield Centre, CT: Martino. (Original work published in 1930)

Friel, J. C., & Friel, L. D. (2010). *Adult children: Secrets of dysfunctional families.* Deerfield Beach, FL: Health Communications.

Fullagar, S., & O'Brien, W. (2014). Social recovery and the move beyond deficit models of depression: A feminist analysis of mid-life women's self-care practices. *Social Science and Medicine, 117,* 116–124.

Fuller-Thomson, E., Katz, R. B., Phan, V. T., Liddycoat, J. P. M., & Brennenstuhl, S. (2013). The long arm of parental addictions: The association with adult children's depression in a population-based study. *Psychiatry Research, 210,* 95–101.

Gabbard, G. O. (1993). On hate in love relationships: The narcissism of minor differences revisited. *The Psychoanalytic Quarterly, 62,* 229–238.

Gayman, M. D., Cislo, A. M., Goidel, A. R., & Ueno, K. (2014). SES and race ethnic differences in the stress buffering effects of coping resources among young adults. *Ethnicity and Health, 19,* 198–216.

Gladding, S. T. (2014). *Family therapy: History, theory and practice* (6th ed.). Upper Saddle River, NJ: Pearson.

Goebert, D., & Nishimura, S. (2011). Comparison of substance abuse treatment utilization and preferences among Native Hawaiians, Asian Americans and Euro Americans. *Journal of Substance Use, 16,* 161–170.

Goodman, S. (n.d.). *Psychodynamic approach to addiction treatment.* Retrieved from http://www.researchgate.net/publictopics.PublicPostFileLoader.html?id=53a74a6ed685cc61708b45e1&key=e022204e-4819-44de-8737-9722f6baaa33

Green, K. E., & Feinstein, B. A. (2012). Substance use in lesbian, gay, and bisexual populations: An update on empirical research and implications for treatment. *Psychology of Addictive Behaviors, 26,* 265–278.

Griffiths, M. (2005). A "components" model of addiction within a biopsychosocial framework. *Journal of Substance Use, 10,* 191–197.

Haley, J., & Richeport-Haley, M. (2007). *Directive family therapy.* New York, NY: Haworth Press.

Haller, M. (2013). Disentangling the directions of influence among trauma exposure, post traumatic stress disorder symptoms, and alcohol and drug problems. *Dissertation Abstracts International: Section B. The Sciences and Engineering, 74*(4-B)(E).

Hammack, S. E., Cooper, M. A., & Lexak, K. R. (2012). Overlapping neurobiology of learned helplessness and conditioned defeat: Implications for PTSD and mood disorders. *Neuropharmacology, 62,* 565–575.

Hardee, J. E., Welland, B. J., Nichols, T. E., Welsh, R. C., Soules, M. E., Steinberg, D. B., . . . & Heitzeg, M. M. (2014). Development of impulse control circuitry in children of alcoholics. *Biological Psychiatry, 76,* 708–716.

Harkness, D. (2001). Testing Cermak's hypothesis: Is dissociation the mediating variable that links substance abuse in the family of origin with offspring codependency? *Journal of Psychoactive Drugs, 22,* 75–82.

Hasin, D. S., O'Brien, C. P., Auriacombe, M., Borges, G., Bucholz, K., Budney, A., . . . & Grant, B. F. (2012). *DSM-5* criteria for substance use disorders: Recommendations and rationale. *The American Journal of Psychiatry, 170,* 834–851.

Hazeldon Betty Ford Foundation. (n.d.-a). *Helping families when a loved one has addiction.* Retrieved from http://www.hazelden.org/web/public/friends_family.page

Hazeldon Betty Ford Foundation. (n.d.-b). *Payoff matrix helps clients make changes.* Retrieved from http://www.bhevolution.org/public/payoffmatrix.page

Hearn, J., & Lawrence, M. (1985). Family sculpting: Some practical examples. *Journal of Family Therapy, 7,* 113–131.

Hecht, M. L., Collier, M. J., & Ribeau, S. A. (1993). *African American communication: Ethnic identity and cultural interpretation.* Thousand Oaks, CA: Sage.

Hecker, L. L. (2014). *An introduction to marriage and family therapy.* Hoboken, NJ: Taylor & Francis.

Hedges, K. E. (2012). A family affair: Contextual accounts of addicted youth growing up in substance using families. *Journal of Youth Studies, 15,* 257–272.

Heppner, W. L., Kemis, M. H., Nexlek, J. B., Foster, J., Lakey, C. E., & Goldman, B. M. (2008). Within-person relationships among daily self-esteem, need satisfaction, and authenticity. *Psychological Science, 19,* 1140–1145.

Hesse, M. (2006). The readiness ruler as a measure of readiness to change poly-drug use in drug abusers. *Harm Reduction Journal, 3,* 1–5. doi:10.1186/1477-7517-3-3

Heyman, G. M. (2013). Addiction and choice: Theory and new data. *Frontiers in Psychiatry, 4,* 31. doi:10.3389/fpsyt.2013.00031

Hinrichs, J., DeFife, J., & Westen, D. (2011). Personality subtypes in adolescent and adult children of alcoholics: A two part study. *Journal of Nervous and Mental Disease, 199,* 487–498.

Hinson, R., & Rehm, J. (2013). Measuring the burden: Alcohol's evolving impact. *Alcohol Research: Current Reviews, 35,* 122–127.

Hoggard, L. S., Byrd, C. M., & Sellers, R. M. (2012). Comparison of African American college students' coping with racially and nonracial stressful events. *Cultural Diversity and Ethnic Minority Psychology, 18,* 329–339.

Hopsicker, R. J. (2014). The impact of parenting interventions on family functioning for women in residential substance abuse treatment. *Dissertation Abstracts International: Section B. The Sciences and Engineering, 75*(3-B)(E).

Hughes, T. L., & Eliason, M. (2002). Substance use and abuse in lesbian and transgender populations. *The Journal of Primary Prevention, 22,* 263–298.

Hussong, A. M., Bauer, D. J., Huang, W., Chassin, L., Sher, K. J., & Zucker, R. A. (2008). Characterizing the life stressors of children of alcoholic parents. *Journal of Family Psychology, 22,* 819–832.

Hussong, A. M., & Chassin, L. (2004). Stress and cooping among children of alcoholic parents through the young adult transition. *Development and Psychopathology, 16,* 985–1006.

Hussong, A. M., Zucker, R. A., Wong, M. M., Fitzgerald, H. E., & Puttler L. I. (2005). Social competence in children of alcoholic parents over time. *Developmental Psychology, 41,* 747–759.

Ingram, R. E., Atchley, R. A., & Segal, Z. V. (2011). *Vulnerability to depression: From cognitive neuroscience to prevention and treatment.* New York, NY: Guilford Press.

Jann, M., Kennedy, W. K., & Lopez, G. (2014). Benzodiazepines: A major component in unintentional prescription drug overdoses with opioid analgesics. *Journal of Pharmacy Practice, 27,* 5–16.

Johnson, B. (2013). Addiction and will. *Frontiers in Human Neuroscience, 7,* 545.

Jones, J. D., Mogali, S., & Comer, S. D. (2012). Polydrug abuse: A review of opioid and benzodiazepine combination use. *Drug and Alcohol Dependence, 125,* 8–18.

Jordan, K., & Shaw, R. (2008). Object relations theory in family therapy. In K. Shaw (Ed.), *The quick theory reference guide: A resource for expert and novice mental health professionals* (pp. 209–225). Hauppauge, NY: Nova Science.

Kachadourian, L. K., Pilver, C. E., & Potenza, M. N. (2014). Trauma, PTSD, and binge and hazardous drinking among women and men: Findings from a national study. *Journal of Psychiatric Research, 55,* 35–43.

Kelley, M. L., Braitman, A., Henson, J. M., Schroeder, V., Ladage, J., & Gumienny, L. (2010). Relationships among depressive mood symptoms and parent and peer relations in collegiate children of alcoholics. *American Journal of Orthopsychiatry, 80,* 204–212.

Kimble, M., Boxwala, M., Bean, W., Maletsky, K., Halper, J., Spollen, K., & Fleming, K. (2014). The impact of hypervigilance: Evidence for a forward feedback loop. *Journal of Anxiety Disorders, 28,* 241–245.

Klostermann, K., Chen, R., Kelley, M. L., Schroeder, V. M., Braitman, A. L., & Mignone, T. (2011). Coping behavior and depressive symptoms in adult children of alcoholics. *Substance Use and Misuse, 46,* 1162–1168.

Koob, G. F., & Le Moal, M. (2008). Addiction and the brain antireward system. *Annual Reviews: Psychology, 59,* 29–53.

Kopera, M., Glass, J. M., Heitzeg, M. M., Wojnar, M., Puttlier, L. I., & Zucker, R. A. (2014). Theory of mind among young adult children from alcoholic families. *Journal of Studies on Alcohol and Drugs, 75,* 889–894.

Kunimatsu, M. M., & Marsee, M. A. (2012). Examining the presence of anxiety in aggressive individuals: The illuminating role of fight or flight mechanisms. *Child and Youth Care Forum, 41,* 247–258.

Kuo, J. R., Khoury, J. E., Metcalf, R., Fitzpatrick, S., & Goodwill, A. (2014). An examination of the relationship between childhood emotional abuse and borderline personality disorder features: The role of difficulties with emotional regulation. *Child Abuse and Neglect, 39,* 147–155.

Lalonde, B., Rabinowitz, P., Shefsky, M. L., & Washienko, K. (1997). La esperanza del valle: Alcohol prevention novelas for Hispanic youth and their families. *Health Education & Behavior, 24,* 587–602.

Lang, P. J., McTeague, L. M., & Bradley, M. M. (2014). Pathological anxiety and function/dysfunction in the brain's fear/defense circuitry. *Restorative Neurology and Neuroscience, 32,* 63–77.

Larsen, E. (1985). *Stage II recovery: Life beyond addiction.* Minneapolis, MN: Winston Press.

Larson, J. H., Holt, B., Wilson, S. M., Medora, N., & Newell, K. (2001). Dating behaviors, attitudes, and relationships satisfaction of young adult children of alcoholics. *Alcoholism Treatment Quarterly, 19,* 1–18.

Lecompte, V., Moss, E., Cyr, C., & Pascuzzo, K. (2014). Preschool attachment, self-esteem and the development of preadolescent anxiety and depressive symptoms. *Attachment and Human Development, 16,* 242–260.

Legha, R., Raleigh-Cohn, A., Fickenscher, A., & Novins, D. (2014). Challenges to providing substance abuse treatment services for American Indian and Alaska native communities: Perspectives of staff from 18 treatment centers. *BMC Psychiatry, 14,* 248–266. doi:10.1186/1471-244X-14-181

Leipman, M. R., Flachier, R., & Tareen, R. S. (2012). Family behavior loop mapping: A technique to analyze the grip addictive disorders have on families and help them recover. In O. J. Morgan & C. H. Litzke (Eds.), *Family intervention in substance abuse: Current best practices* (pp. 59–80). New York, NY: Routledge.

Leipman, M. R., Nirenberg, T. D., Doolittle, R. H., Broffman, T. E., & Sylvia, L. Y. (1993). *Alcoholism relapse may provide advantages to families.* Bethesda, MD: AMERSA National Conference.

LePoire, B. A. (2004). The influence of drugs and alcohol on family communication: The effects that substance abuse has on family members and the effects that family members have on substance abuse. In A. L. Vangelisti (Ed.), *Handbook of communication* (pp. 609–628). Mahwah, NJ: Erlbaum.

Leyton, M. (2013). Are addictions diseases or choices? *Journal of Psychiatry and Neuroscience, 38,* 219–221.

Liota, J. (2012). *Delaying the crossroads: The impact of parental alcoholism on self-authorship.* Retrieved from Indiana University Student Personnel Association website: http://scholarworks.iu.edu/journals/index.php/jiuspa/article/view/1349/1952

Love Longman, T. R. (2014). Adult children of drug abuse: Levels of psychopathology in comparison to adult children of alcoholics and controls. *Dissertation Abstracts International: Section B. The Sciences and Engineering, 75*(1-B)(E).

Macaskill, A., & Denovan, A. (2014). Assessing psychological health: The contribution of psychological strengths. *British Journal of Guidance & Counselling, 42,* 320–337.

MacGowan, M. (2006). Measuring and increasing engagement in substance abuse treatment groups: Advancing evidence-based group work. *Journal of Groups in Addiction and Recovery, 1,* 53–67.

Madanes, C. (1981). *Strategic family therapy.* San Francisco, CA: Jossey-Bass.

Maslow, A. H. (1969). A theory of metamotivation: The biological rooting of the value-life. *Humanitas, 4,* 301–343.

Mares, S. H. W., van der Vorst, H., Engels, R., & Lichtwarck-Aschoff, A. (2011). Parental alcohol use, alcohol-related problems, alcohol-specific attitudes, alcohol-specific communication, and adolescent excessive alcohol use and alcohol-related problems: An indirect path model. *Addictive Behaviors, 36,* 209–216.

Marrett, K. M., Sprenkle, D. H., & Lewis, R. A. (1992). Family members' perceptions of family boundaries and their relationship to family problems. *Family Therapy, 19,* 233–242.

Mate, G. (2010). *In the realm of hungry ghosts: Close encounters with addiction.* Berkeley, CA: North Atlantic Books

Matsumoto, K., Pinna, G., Puia, G., Guidotti, A., & Costa, E. (2005). Social isolation stress-induced aggression in mice: A model to study the pharmacology of neurosteroidogenesis. *Stress, 8,* 85–93.

Matto, H. C., Brown, S., & Ballan, M. S. (2014). Substance abuse. In H. C. Matto, J. Strolin-Goltzman, & M. S. Ballan (Eds.), *Neuroscience for social work: Current research and practice* (pp. 217–234). New York, NY: Springer.

McDonald, B. K. (2013). *Out of the mirror: A workbook for healing adult children of covert narcissists: A literature review and experiential project*. Retrieved from http://www.alfredadler.edu/sites/default/files/McDonald%20MP%202013.pdf

McGoldrick, M., Giordano, J., & Garcia-Preto, N. (2005). *Ethnicity & family therapy* (3rd ed.). New York, NY: Guilford Press.

McIlveen, J. W. (2014). The relationship between parental lifestyle, attachment style and the mediating effect of family environment on the characteristics of their adult children in substance abuse treatment. *Dissertation Abstracts International: Section B. The Sciences and Engineering, 74*(11-B)(E).

Meichenbaum, D. (1977). *Cognitive behavior modification: An integrative approach*. New York, NY: Plenum Press.

Menees, M. M., & Segrin, C. (2000). The specificity of disrupted process in families of adult children of alcoholics. *Alcohol and Alcoholism, 35*, 361–367.

Mersky, J. P. (2008). Review of impact of substance abuse on children and families: Research and practice implications. *Journal of Social Work Practice in the Addictions, 8*, 550–552.

Meyer, I. H., & Frost, D. (2003). Minority stress and the health of sexual minorities. In C. J. Patterson & A. R. D'Augelli (Eds.), *Handbook of psychology and sexual orientation* (pp. 252–266). New York, NY: Oxford University Press.

Middleton-Moz, J., & Dwinell, L. (2010). *After the tears: Helping adult children of alcoholics heal their childhood trauma*. Deerfield Beach, FL: Health Communications.

Mikulincer, M., Shaver, P. R., Bar-On, N., & Sahdra, B. K. (2014). Security attachment, self-esteem threat, and mental depletion affect provision of a safe haven and secure base to a romantic partner. *Journal of Social and Personal Relationships, 31*, 630–650.

Miller, W. R. (1983). Motivational interviewing with problem drinkers. *Behavioural Psychotherapy, 11*, 147–172.

Miller, W. R., & Rollnick, S. (2013). *Motivational interviewing: Helping people change* (3rd ed.). New York, NY: Guilford Press.

Minuchin, S. (1974). *Families and family therapy*. Cambridge, MA: Harvard University Press.

Minuchin, S. (2006). *Mastering family therapy: Journeys of growth and transformation*. Hoboken, NJ: Wiley.

Moore, B. C., Biegel, D. E., & McMahon, T. J. (2011). Maladaptive coping as a mediator of family stress. *Journal of Social Work Practice in the Addictions, 11*, 17–39.

National Council on Alcoholism and Drug Dependence (NCADD). (n.d.-a). *Alcohol and drug abuse affects everyone in the family.* Retrieved from http://www.ncadd.org/index.php/get-help/family-information-and-education

National Council on Alcoholism and Drug Dependence. (NCADD). (n.d.-b). *Alcohol & drug information.* Retrieved from http://www.ncadd.org/index.php/for-the-media/alcohol-a-drug-information

National Council on Alcoholism and Drug Dependence (NCADD). (n.d.-c). *FAQs/Facts.* Retrieved from http://ncadd.org/index.php/learn-about-drugs/faqsfacts/209-drugs-faqs-facts?format=phocapdf

National Institute on Alcohol Abuse and Alcoholism. (n.d.). Retrieved from http://www.niaaa.nih.gov

National Institute on Drug Abuse. (n.d.). *Is marijuana addictive?* Retrieved from http://www.drugabuse.gov/publications/research-reports/marijuana/marijuana-addictive

National Institute on Drug Abuse. (2009). *DrugFacts: Hallucinogens–LSD, peyote, psilocybin, and PCP.* Retrieved from http://www.drugabuse.gov/publications/drugfacts/hallucinogens-lsd-peyote-psilocybin-pcp

National Institute on Drug Abuse. (2012a). *Principles of drug addiction treatment: A research-based guide* (3rd ed.). Retrieved from http://www.drugabuse.gov/publications/principles-drug-addiction-treatment-research-based-guide-third-edition/evidence-based-approaches-to-drug-addiction-treatment/behavioral-0

National Institute on Drug Abuse. (2012b). *What are inhalants?* Retrieved from http://teens.drugabuse.gov/drug-facts/inhalants

National Institute on Drug Abuse. (2013). *Drug facts: Cocaine.* Retrieved from http://www.drugabuse.gov/publications/drugfacts/cocaine

National Institute on Drug Abuse. (2014a). *America's addiction to opioids: Heroin and prescription drug abuse.* Retrieved from http://www.drugabuse.gov/about-nida/legislative-activities/testimony-to-congress/2014/americas-addiction-to-opioids-heroin-prescription-drug-abuse

National Institute on Drug Abuse. (2014b). *Drug facts: Methamphetamine.* Retrieved from http://www.drugabuse.gov/publications/drugfacts/methamphetamine

National Institute on Drug Abuse. (2014c). *Emerging trends.* Retrieved February 16, 2015, from http://www.drugabuse.gov/drugs-abuse/emerging-trends

National Institute on Drug Abuse. (2015). *Emerging trends.* Retrieved February 28, 2015, from http://www.drugabuse.gov/drugs-abuse/emerging-trends

Nievar, M. A., Moske, A. K., Johnson, D. J., & Chen, Q. (2014). Parenting practices in preschool leading to later cognitive competence: A family stress model. *Early Education and Development, 25,* 318–337.

Nikulina, V., Widom, C. S., & Brzustowicz, L. M. (2012). Child abuse and neglect, MAOA, and mental health outcomes: A prospective examination. *Biological Psychiatry, 71,* 350–357.

Niv, N., Wong, E. C., & Hser, Y. (2007). Asian Americans in community-based substance abuse treatment: Service needs, utilization, and outcomes. *Journal of Substance Abuse Treatment, 33,* 313–319.

Norwood, R. (1985). *Women who love too much.* New York, NY: Penguin Putnam.

Nutt, D. J. (2008). Relationship of neurotransmitters to the symptoms of major depressive disorder. *Journal of Clinical Psychiatry, 69,* 4–7.

Obot, I. S., & Anthony, J. C. (2004). Mental health problems in adolescent children of alcohol dependent parents: Epidemiologic research with a nationally representative sample. *Journal of Child and Adolescent Substance Abuse, 13,* 83–96.

Oetting, E. R., & Beauvais, F. (1990). Adolescent drug use: Findings of national and local surveys. *Journal of Consulting and Clinical Psychology, 58,* 385–394.

Otway, L. J., & Carnelley, K. B. (2013). Exploring the associations between adult attachment security and self-actualization and self-transcendence. *Self and Identity, 12,* 217–230.

Park, S., & Schepp, K. G. (2014). A systematic review of research on children of alcoholics: Their inherent resilience and vulnerability. *Journal of Child and Family Studies, 24.* doi:10.1007/s10826-014-9930-7

Park, S., Shibusawa, T., Yoon, S. M., & Son, H. (2010). Characteristics of Chinese and Korean Americans in alcohol treatment for alcohol use disorders: Examining heterogeneity among Asian American subgroups. *Journal of Ethnicity in Substance Abuse, 9,* 128–142.

Payne, M. (2006). *Narrative therapy: An introduction for counselors.* Thousand Oaks, CA: Sage.

Pielage, S. B., Luteijn, F., & Arrindell, W. A. (2005). Adult attachment, intimacy and psychological distress in a clinical and community sample. *Clinical Psychology and Psychotherapy, 12,* 455–464.

Piercy, F. P., & Sprenkle, D. H. (1988). Family therapy theory-building questions. *Journal of Marital and Family Therapy, 14,* 307–309.

Pomini, V., Gournellis, R., Kokkevi, A., Tamaras, V., Papadimitriou, G., & Liappas, J. (2014). Rejection attitudes, poor parental bonding, and stressful life events in heroin addicts' families. *Substance Use and Misuse, 49,* 1867–1877.

Powers, A., Stevens, J., Fami, N., & Bradley, B. (2015). Construct validity of a short self-report instrument assessing emotional dysregulation. *Psychiatry Research, 225,* 85–92.

Prochaska, J. O., DiClemente, C. C., & Norcross, J. C. (2003). In search of how people change: Applications to addictive behaviors. In P. Salovey & A. J. Rothman (Eds.), *Social psychology of health* (pp. 63–77). New York, NY: Psychology Press.

Raffaela, P. (2013). Attachment, locus of control and romantic intimacy in adult children of alcoholics: A correlational investigation. *Dissertation Abstracts International: Section B. The Sciences and Engineering, 74*(6-B)(E).

Rafferty P., & Hartley P. (2006). Shame about the children: A legacy of distress for adults who have grown up with parental problem drinking and family disharmony. *Journal of Substance Use, 11,* 115–127.

Ramisch, J. L., McVicker, M., & Sahin, Z. S. (2009). Helping low-conflict divorced parents establish appropriate boundaries using a variation of the miracle question: An integration of solution-focused therapy and structural family therapy. *Journal of Divorce and Remarriage, 50,* 481–495.

Rangarajan, S. (2008). Mediators and moderators of parental alcoholism effects on offspring self-esteem. *Alcohol and Alcoholism, 43,* 481–491.

Resnicow, K., Soler, R. E., Braithwaite, R. L., Selassie, M. B., & Smith, M. (1999). Development of a racial and ethnic identity scale for African American adolescents: The survey of Black life. *Journal of Black Psychology, 25,* 171–188.

Reyome, N. D., Ward, K. S., & Witklewitz, K. (2010). Relationship between childhood history of emotional maltreatment, codependency and self-silencing. *Journal of Aggression, Maltreatment and Trauma, 19,* 159–179.

Robison, J. (2002a, July 2). *Decades of drug use: Data from the '60s and '70s.* Retrieved from http://www.gallup.com/poll/6331/decades-drug-use-data-from-60s-70s.aspx

Robison, J. (2002b, July 9). *Decades of drug use: Data from the '80s and '90s.* Retrieved from http://www.gallup.com/poll/6352/decades-drug-use-80s-90s.aspx

Rogers, C. (1961). *On becoming a person.* New York, NY: Harcourt.

Rojas, J. I., Hallford, G., Brand, M. W., & Tivis, L. J. (2012). Latino/as in substance abuse treatment: Substance use patterns, family history of addiction, and depression. *Journal of Ethnicity in Substance Abuse, 11,* 75–85.

Rosenberg, M. (1965). *Society and the adolescent self-image.* Princeton, NJ: Princeton University Press.

Sandoz, J. (2004). Codependency? *Annals of the American Psychotherapy Association, 7,* 37–37.

Sansone, R. A., & Sansone, L. A. (2011). Substance use disorders and borderline personality: Common bedfellows. *Innovations in Clinical Neuroscience, 9,* 10–13.

Satir, V. (1994). *Helping families to change.* Lanham, MD: Jason Aronson.

Schuckit, M. A., Smith, T. L., Pierson, J., Trim, R., & Danko, G. P. (2008). Externalizing disorders in the offspring from the San Diego prospective study of alcoholism. *Journal of Psychiatric Research, 42,* 644–652.

Segal, B. (2014). *Perspectives on drug use in the United States*. Hoboken, NJ: Taylor & Francis.

Seif, M. N. (2014). *What every therapist needs to know about anxiety disorders: Key concepts, insights, and interventions*. Hoboken, NJ: Taylor & Francis.

Shaef, A. W. (1986). *Co-dependence: Misunderstood—mistreated*. Minneapolis, MN: Winston Press.

Shame. (n.d.). In *Merriam Webster dictionary online*. Retrieved from http://www.merriam-webster.com/dictionary/shame

Shepherd, L., & Wild, J. (2014). Emotional regulation, physiological arousal and PTSD symptoms in trauma-exposed individuals. *Journal of Behavioral Therapy and Environmental Psychiatry, 45,* 360–367.

Sher, K. J., Walitzer, K. S., Wood, P. K., & Brent, E. E. (1991). Characteristics of children of alcoholics: Putative risk factors, substance use and abuse, and psychopathology. *Journal of Abnormal Psychology, 100,* 427–448.

Singer, J. A., Singer, B. F., & Berry, M. (2013). A meaning-based intervention for addiction: Using narrative therapy and mindfulness to treat alcohol abuse. In J. Hicks & C. Routledge (Eds.), *The experience of meaning in life: Classical perspectives, emerging themes, and controversies* (pp. 379–392). New York, NY: Springer.

Slutske, W. S., D'Onofrio, B. M., Turkheimer, E., Emery, R. E., Harden, K. P., Heath, A. C., & Martin, N. G. (2008). Searching for an environmental effect of parental alcoholism on offspring alcohol use disorder: A genetically informed study of children of alcoholics. *Journal of Abnormal Psychology, 117,* 534–551.

Smith, D. E., & Seymour, R. B. (2001). *Clinician's guide to substance abuse*. Center City, MN: Hazeldon.

Sobell, M. B., & Sobell, L. C. (2008). *Motivational interviewing strategies and techniques: Rationales and examples*. Retrieved from http://www.nova.edu/gsc/forms/mi_rationale_techniques.pdf

Sperry, D. M., & Widom, C. S. (2013). Child abuse and neglect, social support, and psychopathology in adulthood: A prospective investigation. *Child Abuse and Neglect, 37,* 415–425.

Stein, L. A. R., & Rogers R. (2008). Denial and misreporting of substance abuse. In R. Rogers (Ed.), *Clinical assessment of malingering and deception* (pp. 87–108). New York, NY: Guilford Press.

Steinglass, P. (1987). A systems view of family interaction and psychopathology. In T. Jacob (Ed.), *Family interaction and psychopathology: Theories, methods and findings* (pp. 25–65). New York, NY: Plenum Press.

Stevens, P., & Smith, R. (2013). *Substance abuse counseling: Theory and practice* (5th ed.). Upper Saddle River, NJ: Pearson.

Substance Abuse and Mental Health Services Administration. (n.d.). *Racial and ethnic minority populations*. Retrieved from http://www.samhsa.gov/specific-populations/racial-ethnic-minority

Sue, D. W., Arrendondo, P., & McDavis, R. J. (1992). Multicultural competencies and standards: A call to the profession. *Journal of Counseling & Development, 70,* 477–486.

Svrluga, S. (2014, April 22). Fairfax mother of young heroin addict: "There were clues. But we had no clue." *The Washington Post.* Retrieved from http://www.washingtonpost.com/local/fairfax-mother-of-young-heroin-addict-there-were-clues-but-we-had-no-clue/2014/04/22/ab66b03c-b06b-11e3-9627-c65021d6d572_story.html

Swales, M., Heard, H. L., & Williams, J. M. G. (2000). Linehan's dialectical behavior therapy (DBT) for borderline personality disorder: Overview and adaptation. *Journal of Mental Health, 9,* 7–23.

Tackett, S. L., Nelson, L. J., & Busby, D. M. (2013). Shyness and relationship satisfaction: Evaluating the relationships between shyness, self-esteem, and relationship satisfaction in couples. *American Journal of Family Therapy, 41,* 34–45.

Tafa, M., & Baiocco, R. (2009). Addictive behavior and family functioning during adolescence. *American Journal of Family Therapy, 37,* 388–395.

Teodorescu, K., & Erev, I. (2014). Learned helplessness and learned prevalence: Exploring the causal relationships among perceived controllability, reward prevalence, and exploration. *Psychological Science, 25,* 1861–1869.

Terrion, J. L. (2015). A communication model of relational pathways into and out of adolescent substance use disorder. *Journal of Child and Adolescent Substance Abuse, 24,* 54–65.

Titelman, P. (2014). *Clinical applications of Bowen family systems theory.* Hoboken, NJ: Taylor & Francis.

Toman, W. (1998). Basics of family structure and sibling position. In M. D. Kahn & K. G. Lewis (Eds.), *Siblings in therapy: Life span and clinical issues* (pp. 46–65). New York, NY: Norton.

Tombs, D. L. (2013). *Introduction to addictive behaviors* (4th ed.). New York, NY: Guilford Press.

Tull, M. (2008). An examination of the fear of bodily sensations and body hypervigilance as predictors of emotion regulation difficulties among individuals with a recent history of uncued panic attacks. *Journal of Anxiety Disorders, 22,* 750–760.

Turner, L. A., & Langhinrichsen-Rohling, J. (2011). Attachment, relationship beliefs, and partner-specific assertiveness and psychological aggression among college students. *Partner Abuse, 2,* 387–403.

Ubinger, M. E., Handal, P. J., & Massura, C. E. (2013). Adolescent adjustment: The hazards of conflict avoidance and the benefits of conflict. *Psychology, 4,* 50–58.

United Nations Office on Drugs and Crime. (2008). *2008 world drug report.* Retrieved from http://www.unodc.org/documents/wdr/WDR_2008/WDR_2008_eng_web.pdf

van Dijke, A., Ford, J. D., van Son, M., Frank, L., & van der Hart, O. (2013). Association of childhood trauma by primary caregiver and affect dysregulation with borderline personality disorder symptoms in adulthood. *Psychological Trauma: Theory, Research, Practice, and Policy, 5,* 217–224.

Van Ryzin, M. J., Fosco, G. M., & Dishion, T. J. (2012). Family and peer predictors of substance use from early adolescence to early adulthood: An 11-year prospective analysis. *Addictive Behaviors, 37,* 1314–1324.

Vela, R. (2014). The effect of severe stress on early brain development, attachment, and emotions: A psychoanatomical formulation. *Psychiatric Clinics of North America, 37,* 519–534.

Vernig, P. M. (2011). Family roles with alcohol-dependent parents: An evidence-based review. *Substance Use and Misuse, 46,* 535–542.

Vigilance. (n.d.). In *Merriam Webster dictionary online.* Retrieved from http://www.merriam-webster.com/dictionary/vigilant

Volkow, N. D., Wang, G., Fowler, J. S., & Tomasi, D. (2012). Addiction circuitry in the human brain. *Annual Reviews: Pharmacology and Toxicology, 52,* 321–336.

Walters, S. T., & Rotgers, F. (Eds.). (2012). *Treating substance abuse: Theory and technique* (3rd ed.). New York, NY: Guilford Press.

WebMD. (n.d.). *Benzodiazepine abuse.* Retrieved from http://www.webmd.com/mental-health/addiction/benzodiazepine-abuse?page=4

Wegscheider-Cruse, S. (Ed.). (1989). *Another chance: Hope and health for the alcoholic family.* Pompano Beach, FL: Communications.

Wells, M. C., Hill, M. B., Brack, C. J., & Firestone, E. E. (2006). Codependency's relationship to defining characteristics in college students. *Journal of College Student Psychotherapy, 20,* 71–84.

Whitaker, C. (1982). *From psyche to systems: The evolving therapy of Carl Whitaker.* New York, NY: Guilford Press.

Whitfield, C. L. (1987). *Healing the child within: Discovery and recovery for adult children of dysfunctional families.* Deerfield Beach, FL: Health Communications.

Wilens, T. E., Yule, A., Martelon, M., Zulauf, C., & Faraone, S. V. (2014). Parental history of substance use disorders (SUD) and SUD in offspring: A controlled family study of bipolar disorder. *The American Journal on Addictions, 25,* 440–446.

Williams, L., & Jimenez, M. (2012). Treating the overfunctioning and underfunctioning couple. *Journal of Family Therapy, 40,* 141–151.

Woitiz, J. G. (1983). *Adult children of alcoholics.* Deerfield Beach, FL: Health Communications.

Yalom, I. (2005). *The theory and practice of group psychotherapy* (5th ed.). New York, NY: Basic Books.

Yendork, J. S., & Somhlaba, N. Z. (2014). Stress, coping and quality of life: An exploratory study of the psychological well-being of Ghanian orphans placed in orphanages. *Children and Youth Services Review, 46,* 28–37.

Young, C. B., Fang, D. Z., & Zisook, S (2010). Depression in Asian American and Caucasian undergraduate students. *Academic Psychiatry, 36,* 11–16.

Young, C. F., & Skorga, P. (2013). Collaborative care for depression and anxiety problems. *International Journal of Evidence-Based Healthcare, 11,* 341–343.

Yudofsky, S. C. (2012). *Clinical manual of neuropsychiatry.* Washington, DC: American Psychiatric Publishing.

INDEX

Figures and tables are indicated by "f" and "t" following the page numbers.